DUELS OF THE MIND

THE TWELVE BEST GAMES OF CHESS

DUELS OF THE MIND

THE TWELVE BEST GAMES OF CHESS

Selected by

Raymond Keene

COLLIER BOOKS
MACMILLAN PUBLISHING COMPANY
NEW YORK

Maxwell Macmillan Canada
Toronto

Collier Books
Macmillan Publishing Company
866 Third Avenue, New York, NY 10022

Maxwell Macmillan Canada, Inc.
1200 Eglinton Avenue East, Suite 200
Don Mills, Ontario M3C 3N1

Library of Congress Cataloging-in-Publication Data

Keene, Raymond D.
    Duels of the Mind: the twelve best games of chess
  by Raymond Keene.—1st Collier Books ed.
        p.   cm.
    ISBN 0–02–028701–1
    1. Chess—Collections of games.   2. Chess—Tournaments.
  I. Title.
  GV1452.K37   1991   9C–27161   CIP
  794.1′52—dc20

Macmillan books are available at special discounts for bulk
purchases for sales promotions, premiums, fund-raising, or
educational use. For details, contact:
        Special Sales Director
        Macmillan Publishing Company
        866 Third Avenue
        New York, NY 10022

First Collier Books Edition 1991

10 9 8 7 6 5 4 3 2 1

Printed in Great Britain

CONTENTS

FOREWORD 7

HOW TO USE THIS BOOK 9
Notation
Layout
Diagrams
Rates of Exchange

INTRODUCTION 12

1 THE DAWN OF TOURNAMENT PLAY 15
Anderssen–Kieseritsky (London 1851)
The King's Gambit

2 PAUL MORPHY, THE AMERICAN METEOR 21
Paulsen–Morphy (New York 1857)

3 THE FIEND HAS OFFERED HIS QUEEN 27
Zukertort–Blackburne (London 1883)
Flank Openings: 1 c4 and 1 ♘f3

Contents

4   **A Champagne Victory**   34
Steinitz–Tchigorin (Havana 1892)
Ruy Lopez

5   **Battle of Titans**   41
Pillsbury–Lasker (St Petersburg 1896)
The Queen's Gambit

6   **The Thunderbolt**   49
Bernstein–Capablanca (Moscow 1914)

7   **The Marshal's Baton**   55
Bogolyubov–Alekhine (Hastings 1922)

8   **Paralysis**   63
Sämisch–Nimzowitsch (Copenhagen 1923)
Indian Defences

9   **Russian Revolution**   69
Botvinnik–Capablanca (Rotterdam 1938)

10   **The Rampant Rook**   77
Larsen–Spassky (Belgrade 1970)

11   **A Mozart Symphony**   81
Fischer–Spassky (Reykjavik 1972)

12   **Star Wars**   89
Karpov–Kasparov (Moscow 1985)
The Sicilian Defence

List of Illustrations   96

FOREWORD

Donald Woods

Duels Of The Mind is a great title for a great chess book and it is a real privilege to be invited to write this Foreword, as it was to help Grandmaster Raymond Keene present his fine Thames Television series on these Twelve Best Games Of Chess. In the international sphere of the game he needs no introduction: his role in helping to spark the renaissance of British chess – to the stage where Britain is now second only to the Soviet Union in the chess world – speaks for itself. Ray was a hero of mine before we met, his authoritative book on the King's Indian Defence being a constant resource ever since I became a compulsive King's Indian devotee.

But our first meeting, at the South Africa Open in Cape Town in 1976, was a severe disillusionment for me. My board was in the centre of a sea of tables for the ordinary players, while Ray was up on a platform behind velvet ropes in the Grandmasters and Superstars enclosure, and I hoped I'd get a chance during the tournament to ask him to autograph my King's Indian book. Imagine my elation, therefore, when during the course of play Raymond several times wandered down through the throng and directly to my table, evincing considerable interest in my game. 'By gad', I thought (or the South African equivalent), 'I must have something going here . . . Keene himself is fascinated by it'. Inspired by this grandmasterly approbation I won my game, then assumed what I hoped was a suitably modest expression as I went to him for his autograph. 'You could have won five moves earlier,' he remarked abstractedly, adding with considerably more animation: 'I came over to your table hoping to discuss your article in today's *Cape Times*'. Damn; it had had nothing to do with my chess after all!

We next met at the FIDE congress in Lucerne in 1977, where I was a delegate for the South African Chess Federation, trying to head off a Soviet bloc move to expel us over apartheid. In those days I was still opposed to boycotts, and Ray and other chess notables from the West were steadfast in our support as we in the SACF were also anti-apartheid. In the event we lost the vote by a narrow margin, but the Nigerian delegate's speech made a deep impression on me and started me thinking there could be a case for the boycott. In essence his argument was that while apartheid in general lasted no black chess player in South Africa could have an equal chance against a white player because of the inferior nutrition, education, living standards and general restrictions on the blacks in all spheres of life. In the circumstances opening chess clubs up to black members was simply not enough to solve the overall problem. A few months later back in South Africa my close friend Steve Biko was killed by the Security Police and for publicising what had happened to him I was arrested and banned by the South African government. In chess terms this was okay, because whatever the disadvantages of this form of house arrest it is good for one's hobbies, and as I was allowed the company of one person at a time several steadfast members of my chess club came to my house in relays to play, ignoring the intimidatory notings of their identities and car numberplates by the Security Police.

Eventually I escaped with my family to Britain in January 1978, shortly thereafter receiving a moving salute by Ray in the dedication to me of his book on the Korchnoi–Spassky match, and a further compliment was that he emulated my conversion to the boycott principle on the South African issue. He has remained a loyal supporter of this stand ever since, which to a leading professional means real financial sacrifice. After twelve years we are both glad that the encouraging developments in South Africa spur the hope of the prospective re-entry of South Africa into international chess once apartheid is totally abolished.

So I write this Foreword not only as a friend and chess disciple of Ray's, but as an admirer of his political principles as well where my country is concerned. Hopefully we will both be able to compete again in another South African Open one of these days, and if he wanders over to my table I won't repeat the mistake of thinking his interest is sparked by my masterly deployment of the King's Indian!

I hope readers will enjoy the presentation of these twelve great games as much as I have enjoyed helping Ray in his analysis and commentary on Thames Television. Each of the games has its own fascination, from the paralysing constriction by Nimzowitsch in the Immortal Zugzwang to the nuclear destruction of Karpov's pieces in what is herein dubbed Star Wars.

So on with your clocks – and may the Force be with you!

Donald Woods
London 1991

HOW TO USE THIS BOOK

Notation

The moves to all twelve of the games contained in this book are given in what is known as 'Figurine Algebraic Notation'. This somewhat complicated-sounding term actually describes a very simple way of writing down the moves. Readers familiar with the system can jump ahead to the games themselves, but those who are comparatively new to the game or who have only learned the older English Descriptive notation will find what follows helpful. It is assumed that the reader knows how to play chess.

Each piece is represented by a symbol, called a 'Figurine', as follows:

Pawn ♙

Knight ♘

Bishop ♗

Rook ♖

Queen ♕

King ♔

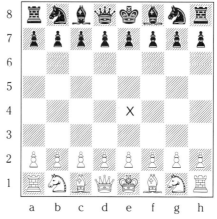

The squares on the chessboard are described by a letter and a number (see diagram A). For instance the square marked with a cross is called 'e4'.

To write down a move, first of all a figurine is given, followed by the square to which that piece moves. Thus, in the diagram, '1 ♘f3' means that on White's first move he has moved his knight from g1 to f3. Occasionally, more than one similar piece can go to a given square. In such cases, information is also given about the departure square, e.g. '8 ♖ad1' indicates that the white rook standing on the a-file (at a1) moves to d1.

Pawn moves omit the figurine. '1 ... d5' therefore means that Black moves the pawn on d7 to d5. The three dots indicate that this was a move by Black.

Captures are indicated by a 'x' symbol; for instance '17 ♗xg7' indicates that White captured something on g7 with a bishop on move 17.

Castling on the kingside is indicated by 0–0.

Castling on the queenside is indicated by 0–0–0.

En passant pawn captures are given as though the captured pawn had moved only one square. For instance, if Black moves a pawn from f7 to f5, next to a white pawn at g5, which then captures the f-pawn, the move is given as 'gxf6', i.e. exactly as if Black had moved the f-pawn to f6 instead of f5.

Various other symbols are used:

+	Check
!	Strong move
!!	Brilliant move
?	Bad move
??	Blunder
!?	Interesting move
?!	Dubious move

Other, more abstruse, symbols are used in many chess books, but not here.

Layout

Moves can be laid out in two ways: either in columns or as ordinary text. In this book, the moves of the twelve main games are all given in columns, thus:

1	e4	e5
2	♘f3	♘c6
3	♗b5	a6

... and so on. Notes or subsidiary games are written as text, so that the three moves above would be written: 1 e4 e5 2 ♘f3 ♘c6 3 ♗b5 a6 etc.

Diagrams

To assist readers unused to Algebraic notation, the letters a–h and the numbers 1–8 are printed alongside the diagrams.

To the top left of each diagram there is a number and a letter (either '*W*' or '*B*'). The number is simply the diagram number, while the letter tells you whose turn it is to move next in the diagram.

Rates of Exchange

Inexperienced players will find the following table helpful. It gives the relative values of the pieces, and will help you to understand why certain moves are described as 'sacrifices' or as 'winning material'.

Piece	*Value*
Pawn	1
Knight	3
Bishop	3
Rook	5
Queen	9
King	Priceless

Thus, a player will rarely be happy to give up a queen for a rook, but will usually be willing to exchange bishop for knight. Many other factors will come into consideration when deciding about captures, and the values given can fluctuate dramatically during the course of a game.

I approve strongly of rational games
for they serve to perfect the art of thinking
LEIBNITZ

Chess, the touchstone of the intellect
GOETHE

INTRODUCTION

S INCE THE ninth century AD, prowess at chess has been regarded as one of the prime indications of intellectual achievement. Chess as a game has developed in the intervening centuries into a highly competitive modern sport, while at the same time exhibiting qualities of artistic creation. The advance of the science and knowledge of chess has also mirrored intellectual achievements in other spheres of human activity, such as painting, literature and music.

In this book, I will be presenting to you the 12 best games of chess ever played. They are games which witness brilliant master strokes of chessboard genius, games which often heralded the decisive onset of a conquering new champion, or even decided the fate of the World Championship itself. I hope they convey to you, the readers, as powerfully as they have done to me, the sense of intellectual mystery and mental force which we associate with chess at its finest.

The games range from London 1851, when competitive chess was in its infancy, via the tournament at New York in 1857, the very first official chess event held in the New World, back to London of the 1880s, when the capital was at the height of its imperial glory. We see, in 1892, the World Championship decided between two European Grandmasters in the tropical heat of Havana. In pre-revolutionary St Petersburg we witness the confirmation of a new champion, Emanuel Lasker, the man who was to reign a record-breaking 27 years, while at Moscow on the eve of a conflagration which was to engulf the civilised world, we witness the Cuban genius, Capablanca, hurl a thunderbolt so devastating that chess fans today will find its depths astounding.

A new generation will be depicted after the carnage of the First World War. Displaced Russian emigrés, such as Alekhine, Bogolyubov, and Nimzowitsch, players impregnated with the twisted logic of four years of mass murder on European battlefields. These were Grandmasters whose play was enigmatic and discordant by classical standards, whose artistic creations reflected in chess terms the artistic exploration of Picasso, Kafka and Stravinsky in other realms of human endeavour.

Finally, we pass across the decades of Soviet domination, represented by Botvinnik and Spassky. This was broken solely and briefly by the temperamental American genius Bobby Fischer in 1972. Sadly, since then, the mercurial American has not played a serious game of chess. I conclude with a taste of the marathon struggle for world chess supremacy that has lasted for half a decade between Anatoly Karpov and Gary Kasparov. Perhaps the most dramatic game in this series is the one that catapulted Kasparov to becoming, at the age of 22, the youngest World Champion in the history of chess.

Before we begin our colourful journey through chess history, I would like to acknowledge the assistance of Keith Mosedale, Executive Producer at Thames Television, Lewis Williams, Director of the *Duels of the Mind* TV series and Dr. Jacqueline Eales, who helped with historical research.

1

■ ■

THE DAWN OF TOURNAMENT PLAY

Anderssen–Kieseritsky (London 1851)

THE IDEA to hold the very first international chess tournament was born in London in 1851. The tournament was designed to coincide with the Great Exhibition, the lavish showcase of Queen Victoria's vast empire, staged to demonstrate British might and industrial progress to the world. Joseph Paxton's plan for the Crystal Palace, which housed the Exhibition, defeated 233 other designs and was first presented to the public on the pages of the *Illustrated London News*. The London 1851 chess tournament was organised by the foremost player of the age, Howard Staunton, also, coincidentally, the chess correspondent of the *Illustrated London News*. His match victory over the Frenchman, St Amant, in 1843, had given him the equivalent of World Champion status, although formal recognition of such a title was still some way in the future.

Staunton's career was typical of the exuberant self-confidence of the Victorian Age. By his own account he was the illegitimate son of Frederick Howard, fifth Earl of Carlisle. If this was so, he nevertheless had to make his own way in the world, first as a chess player and prolific author of chess books, and later in life as a distinguished Shakespearean scholar. Part of his correspondence with Sir Frederic Madden, head of the manuscript department in the British Museum, survives in the Museum today. Together they projected a history of chess in the Middle Ages, but this work was never

Adolph Anderssen

completed. Staunton also published *The Great Schools of England*, an account of the English Public School, the training ground for the administrators of the British Empire.

He was one of the first to recognize the value of commercial endorsement and lent his name to the chess pieces designed by Nathaniel Cooke, a leading craftsman of the period, who, for his pattern for the chess knight, took the magnificent sculptures of horses heads from the Elgin marbles (which Britain had recently acquired) as his inspiration. The Staunton patent chess sets are both elegant and functional and for decades they have been the only ones in use in serious international competitions.

The 1851 tournament crowned Staunton's achievements as a promoter of chess, as he turned his energy and enthusiasm to creating an event which would attract all of Europe's leading players. Sixteen competitors took part in 'a series of grand individual matches' as Staunton grandiosely described his knock-out system. It was won by Adolph Anderssen of Germany, a mathematician, who remained amongst the world's top half dozen players until his death in 1879. Anderssen was a quiet, gentlemanly academic from Breslau, where he lived with his mother and sister, never marrying. He later lost matches to Morphy and Steinitz, but dominated tournaments with victories at London in 1862 and Baden Baden in 1870. He received an honorary doctorate from the University of Breslau in 1865.

Second place to Anderssen in 1851 was taken by the English MP, Marmaduke Wyvill, and third place fell to Elijah Williams, also of England. Staunton took fourth place, an unexpectedly poor showing, but perhaps one that was to be expected, given the great effort that he had expended on organization and in raising a prize fund of £500, an enormous sum for that time. The tournament heralded a new era for international competitive chess. It was the precursor of modern Grandmaster tournaments and of the modern World Championship cycle itself.

The following game, won by Anderssen, was played on the occasion of the 1851 tournament as a 'friendly' game at Simpson's in the Strand, the cigar and coffee Divan so beloved by the chess fraternity of the day. Games there were often played by candlelight. Today Simpson's operates as a restaurant and is still a favourite haunt of chess devotees. Chess pieces adorn its entrance on the Strand and pride of place is given to one of the boards formerly used by Staunton and his contemporaries. In 1851 Anderssen's opponent, Kieseritsky, was an habitué of the Parisian equivalent of Simpson's, the Café de la Régence, where he had installed himself as a chess tutor, giving lessons at 5 francs an hour. He was also the inventor of a three dimensional form of chess, which he utterly failed to make anyone else understand. Kieseritsky had a reputation as a difficult and irritable personality. When he died penniless, he received a pauper's burial and no one attended the grave side.

The vanquished player was so impressed with the brilliant execution of Anderssen's attack that he immediately telegraphed the moves of the game to an awaiting audience at the Café de la Régence. From that day on this sparkling exploit has earned the soubriquet 'The Immortal Game'. Anderssen's triumphs were later recalled during the 1920s, when his imposingly intellectual features decorated German 75 pfennig currency coupons, where the moves and a diagram from the 'Immortal Game' itself also appeared.

White: Anderssen
Black: Kieseritsky
London 1851
KING'S GAMBIT

1	e4	e5
2	f4	exf4
3	♗c4	♛h4+
4	♚f1	b5?!

Bryan's Counter-Gambit, and to modern eyes a very dubious idea. For his pawn Black lures the white bishop from its attacking post and creates an avenue of development for his own queen's bishop on b7. In 1851, even masters regarded this as sufficient compensation for a pawn.

| 5 | ♗xb5 | ♞f6 |
| 6 | ♞f3 | ♛h6 *(1)* |

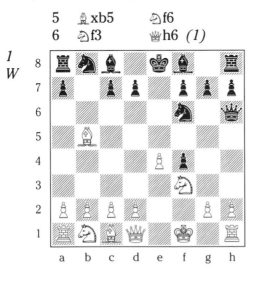

| 7 | d3 | ♞h5 |

Black should have played 7 . . . ♗b7. The transparent threat of . . . ♞g3+ which the text move introduces is parried simply.

8	♞h4	♛g5
9	♞f5	c6
10	g4	♞f6

Better would have been 10 . . . cxb5 11 gxh5 but Black evidently expected to win White's g4 pawn after the hoped-for continuation 11 ♗c4 ♛xg4. Instead of co-operating in this fashion, Anderssen gives up his bishop, the first of many sacrifices in this brilliant game.

| 11 | ♖g1 | cxb5 |
| 12 | h4 | ♛g6 *(2)* |

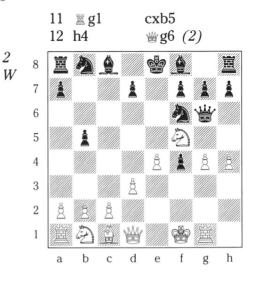

| 13 | h5 | | ♛g5 |
| 14 | ♛f3 | | |

White now has the terrible threat of ♗xf4 trapping Black's queen. In order to create an avenue of escape for the queen, Black has to retreat one of the few pieces he has already developed.

14	...		♞g8
15	♗xf4		♛f6
16	♞c3		♗c5
17	♞d5		

The introduction to a grandiose combination in which White sacrifices both rooks and his queen to deliver checkmate.

| 17 | ... | | ♛xb2 |
| 18 | ♗d6 | | |

Closing the noose around the black king.

| 18 | ... | | ♛xa1+ *(3)* |

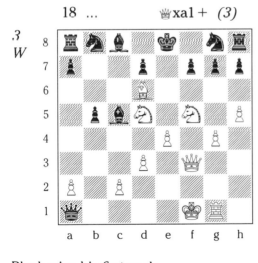

Black wins his first rook.

| 19 | ♚e2 | | ♗xg1 |

Lionel Kieseritsky

Black does not believe White's attack and captures the second rook.

| 20 | e5 | | ♞a6 |
| 21 | ♞xg7+ | | ♚d8 |

Now comes the queen sacrifice to cap all of White's earlier efforts. No wonder this was known as The Immortal Game.

| 22 | ♛f6+!! | | ♞xf6 |
| 23 | ♗e7 *(4)* | | Checkmate. |

The King's Gambit

1 e4 e5 2 f4 – this is the romantic opening par excellence. White gambits a pawn to break open the f-file in order to further his attacking ambitions. Famous practitioners of the gambit include Adolph Anderssen, Bobby Fischer, Boris Spassky and, most recently, Judit Polgar. It was mentioned in the earliest surviving printed work on chess, *Repeticion de Amores y Arte de Axedres* published by Luis Ramirez de Lucena in Spain in 1497.

Lucena's book is divided into two sections, one dealing with chess, the other on love. The chess material includes basic analysis of ten openings (including the King's Gambit), 150 problems and studies and useful practical advice such as: 'Try to play soon after your opponent has eaten or drunk freely.' This kind of tip seemed prevalent in chess literature of the Renaissance, and might be compared with Ruy Lopez on where to place the chessboard. The other side of the coin can be seen in the advice of Carrera in his book: *Il Gioco degli Scacchi* (1617). Carrera suggests this way to prepare for a chess game: 'Abstain some days from meat to clear the brain, as also to let blood . . . take both purgatives and emetics to drive the humours from the body . . . above all be sure to confess sins and receive spiritual absolution just before play in order to counteract the demoniacal influence of magic spells.'

Lucena is also credited with the authorship of the *Göttingen Manuscript*, a 33 page long Latin tract which contains similar material to the *Repeticion*. The section on love is actually an attack on feminism. According to *The Oxford Companion to Chess*, love and chess were both to Lucena, warfare in miniature.

2

■ ■

PAUL MORPHY, THE AMERICAN METEOR

Paulsen–Morphy (New York 1857)

THE AMERICAN genius, Paul Morphy (22nd June 1837–10 July 1884) exploded on to the chess scene in the late 1850s. At the age of 12 Morphy demonstrated his talents in his home town of New Orleans by beating European Master Johann Löwenthal. This established his fame as a prodigy and from then onwards his career had many eerie similarities to that of his twentieth century compatriot, World Champion Bobby Fischer. In 1857 Morphy, at the age of 20, dominated the field in the first American Chess Congress held in New York, where he defeated the German Master Louis Paulsen in the final.

There followed a triumphant tour of London and Paris in which he stormed through European chess, whilst delighting spectators with his casual virtuoso play at blindfold chess, facing up to 8 opponents at a time, without sight of the board. In a series of individual matches, Löwenthal, Harrwitz and Anderssen (the champion of London 1851) suffered dramatic defeats at Morphy's hands. The American's superiority was astounding. Against Anderssen he lost 2 games, drew 2 games, but won 7. His only disappointment was his failure to engage Howard Staunton, who was still the world's most famous player, if not the strongest. Had the World Champion title then existed Morphy would surely have been the holder.

Morphy's exploits were exuberantly fêted in Europe and North America. In Paris a bust was unveiled, and dinners and presentations greeted his return home in

1859. Chess mania gripped America and plans for new clubs, tournaments and books were set in motion. Yet in a curious precursor of Bobby Fischer's withdrawal from public competition after his World Championship victory in 1972, Paul Morphy also chose to retire from serious combat. After his European tour Morphy never again played against first class opponents and confined himself to simultaneous displays or casual games with amateurs, to whom he gave heavy odds.

Chess historian Richard Eales argues that in social terms Morphy's attitude was a throwback to the days when chess skills were regarded as the accomplishments of a gentleman. 'Throughout his life nothing offended Morphy more than the suggestion that chess was a profession or that he wished to profit from playing it'. The early to mid-19th Century had, however, witnessed the development of a corps of players and journalists, who did earn their living from chess activities. Morphy recoiled from this milieu and spent the rest of his life in increasing seclusion. His attempts to set up a legal practice failed and the American civil war damaged the personal fortunes of his family. In later life Morphy sadly developed paranoid delusions and refused even to talk about his former chess triumphs. He died in 1884 after suffering a stroke. As with Bobby Fischer, Morphy's vanishing act at the very height of his powers created a myth of super-human power in the public mind. He played a mere 75 competitive games, but the belief persists that he may have been the greatest genius chess has ever seen.

In terms of chess practice Morphy's contribution was indeed considerable. He was not only well versed in the theory of the day, he was amazingly rapid and accurate in his play. His coruscating technique was ingenious and resourceful. Never blundering, he was also blessed with outstanding understanding of the endgame. As an illustration, I present Morphy's final game against Paulsen in the first American Congress. Paulsen was a distinguished tournament player in the 1860s and 1870s. He was abstemious in the extreme, drinking only water: no tea, coffee or hard liquor passed his lips. He never smoked. He invented the Dragon Variation of the Sicilian Defence and his system has become deservedly popular in modern times. He died, from the complications of diabetes, in 1891. The game which follows illustrates with crystal clarity the overwhelming impact that Morphy's play had on the international chess community of his age.

At this time, before the Staunton patent chess sets had become widely adopted, the more ornate barleycorn pattern of chess set was in general use. It is interesting that the pieces, then, tended to be red and white not black and white, as is now the case. Some feel that these old-style bone pieces are more beautiful than the Staunton design, but they are certainly a lot less functional. The barleycorn pieces were those depicted in Sir John Tenniel's illustrations for Lewis Carroll's chessboard fantasy, *Alice Through the Looking Glass*.

Paul Morphy

White: Paulsen
Black: Morphy
Final, New York Knock-Out Tournament 1857
FOUR KNIGHTS' GAME

1	e4	e5
2	♘f3	♘c6
3	♘c3	♘f6
4	♗b5	♗c5
5	0-0	0-0
6	♘xe5	

This capture introduces a simple exchanging combination known as the 'Fork Trick'. The point is that the reply 6 ... ♘xe5 allows 7 d4 attacking two Black pieces at once.

6	...	♖e8
7	♘xc6	dxc6 *(5)*

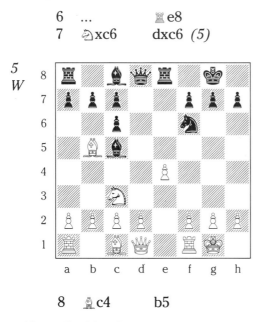

| 8 | ♗c4 | b5 |

Naturally, Morphy, the genius of attack, does not fall for 8 ... ♘xe4, when 9 ♘xe4 ♖xe4 allows 10 ♗xf7 + ♔xf7 11 ♕f3 + with a double attack against Black's king and his rook.

9	♗e2	♘xe4
10	♘xe4	♖xe4
11	♗f3	♖e6
12	c3	

This is a mistake which Morphy is quick to exploit. White should have played 12 d3.

| 12 | ... | ♕d3 |

Now Black's queen occupies a dominating post right in the middle of White's position.

13	b4	♗b6
14	a4	bxa4 *(6)*

15	♕xa4	♗d7
16	♖a2?	

The final slow move which permits Black to launch his annihilating combination, sacrificing his queen to slaughter the white king. It was still not too late to play 16 ♕a6 to challenge the black queen.

24

16 ... ♖ae8
17 ♕a6 ♕xf3‼ (7)

This splendid queen sacrifice must have come as a terrible shock to Paulsen. Black gets just a bishop for his queen, but the important thing is that the g-file is wrenched open, so that Black's rook can join in the onslaught.

18 gxf3 ♖g6+
19 ♚h1 ♗h3
20 ♖d1

If 20 ♖g1, which might look like a more natural defence, then 20 ... ♗g2+ 21 ♖xg2 ♖e1+ 22 ♖g1 ♖exg1 checkmate, a wonderful variation.

20 ... ♗g2+
21 ♚g1 ♗xf3+
22 ♚f1 ♗g2+
23 ♚g1 ♗h3+
24 ♚h1 ♗xf2 (8)

Louis Paulsen

25

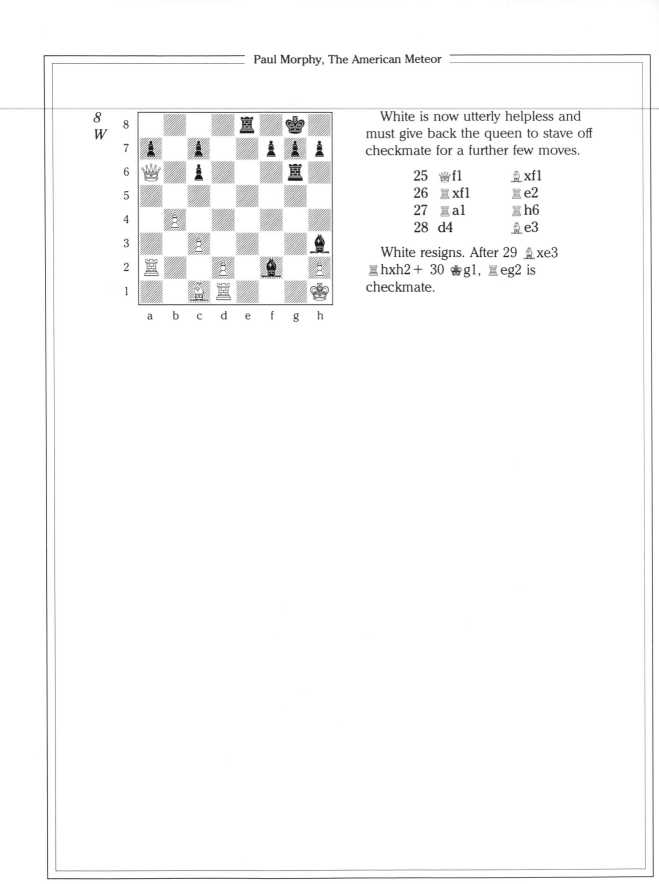

White is now utterly helpless and must give back the queen to stave off checkmate for a further few moves.

25	♕f1	♗xf1
26	♖xf1	♖e2
27	♖a1	♖h6
28	d4	♗e3

White resigns. After 29 ♗xe3 ♖hxh2+ 30 ♔g1, ♖eg2 is checkmate.

3

■ ■

THE FIEND HAS OFFERED HIS QUEEN

Zukertort–Blackburne (London 1883)

THE FIRST official World Championship Match was contested in the cities of New York, St Louis and New Orleans in 1886 between Johannes Zukertort (1842–88) and Wilhelm Steinitz. There had been no official title until that time, but now there was no ambiguity. The match was announced as being 'for the chess championship of the world' and the stakes of $2,000 were the highest ever offered.

Both men had claimed the title before the match, of course! Steinitz argued his own case as early as 1874 when he wrote this about himself in glowingly flattering terms in his chess column in *The Field* magazine: 'Steinitz, who has not yet lost any set match on even terms, and who has come out victorious in the last two international tournaments, London 1872 and Vienna 1873, could claim the title of champion'. While Steinitz was the complete chess professional, Zukertort cut a more flamboyant figure, claiming to be an accomplished soldier, pianist and linguist. His reputation had been made in 1883 at the great London tournament, where he had finished no less than three points ahead of his arch rival Steinitz. In spite of this devastating victory there were already disturbing signs of Zukertort's future mental and physical deterioration. Towards the end of the gruelling London tournament he admitted that he was taking opium to calm his nerves. It was widely believed that as a result the Prussian Master lost his final three games to inferior opponents.

Zukertort started brilliantly in the 1886 showdown with Steinitz, but was the less resilient of the two and ultimately suffered a humiliating loss, winning 5 games, drawing 5 games, but losing ten games. *The Oxford Companion to Chess* describes the terrible effect this defeat had on the loser: 'His spirit crushed, his health failing, Zukertort was advised to give up chess, but there was nothing else he could do. "I am prepared" he said "to be taken away at any moment". Seized by a stroke, while playing at London's famous coffee house, Simpson's Divan, he died next day, aged 46'.

The game I have chosen to illustrate Zukertort's superlative skill was played against Joseph Blackburne, the leading English player, whose competitive daring earned him the title of the 'Black Death' amongst contemporaries. Blackburne was an expert draughts player in his youth, but it was chess that later claimed his devotion and he became a professional player in the late 1860s, achieving excellent tournament results. He earned a living by giving simultaneous displays, touring Britain twice yearly for more than 50 years. He revolutionized the conduct of such events, which had previously been treated as solemn, formal occasions, as if they were scientific

Johannes Zukertort

*The fiend has offered
his Queen and it cannot
be taken without
suffering mate*
Tournament Book,
London 1883

Joseph Blackburne

experiments in the capacities of the human mind. Blackburne preferred to dress in
everyday clothes, to chat and joke as he played and to refresh himself with the odd
glass of whisky. Once he downed his opponent's glass by mistake and remarked 'he
left it *en prise* and I took it *en passant*'.

The game comes from Zukertort's mighty triumph at London 1883, and in the
opinion of many, no more brilliant game of chess had ever been played before. Even
Zukertort's great rival, Steinitz, praised it to the skies, eulogizing 'one of the most noble
combinations conceived over the chess board . . . one of the most brilliant games on
record'.

The tournament itself has the distinction of being the first at which mechanical double chess clocks made an appearance. A time limit on players had first been introduced in 1861 during the Anderssen–Kolisch match in London, when sandglasses were used to calculate the time taken by each side. Independent clocks were used in later events, but the chess clock proper, with its double faces, was perfected in the 1880s by Thomas Bright Wilson of Manchester. Early chess clocks operated on a pendulum system, the modern push button method being introduced at the very end of the 19th century.

The London 1883 tournament was played at the height of the British Empire under the patronage of the Viceroy of India. Opulent chess loving Indian potentates, such as the Maharajah Vizayanagaram, or his Highness the Maharajah of Travancore, followed the Viceroy's lead in lavishing funds on the capital of the empire to attract the world's leading chess masters to display their art. The Indian princes were not disappointed by the result of this sparkling game. The red and white ivory chess set on which the game was played is today in the possession of London chess set collector, Gareth Williams. This red and white ivory set is one of the most artistic examples of the chess set maker's craft. It is now worth many thousands of pounds to collectors.

White: Zukertort
Black: Blackburne
London 1883
FLANK OPENING

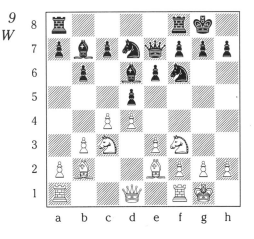

9 W

1	c4	e6
2	e3	♘f6
3	♘f3	b6

A very advanced continuation for 1883.

4	♗e2	♗b7
5	0-0	d5

Equally playable was 5 ... c5, keeping the queen's bishop diagonal open.

6	d4	♗d6
7	♘c3	0-0
8	b3	♘bd7
9	♗b2	♕e7? *(9)*

A positional mistake which surrenders the bishop-pair without satisfactory compensation. Black should have prevented this by playing 9 ... a6 before ... ♕e7. He would then have had a perfectly adequate position.

10	♘b5!	♘e4
11	♘xd6	cd
12	♘d2	

White challenges Black's outpost on e4 in order to facilitate the advance of his central pawns.

12	...	♘df6
13	f3	♘xd2
14	♕xd2	dc
15	♗xc4	

15 bc, of course, does come into consideration. White would then have obtained a powerful pawn centre but his c4 pawn might have become an object of attack.

15	...	d5
16	♗d3	♖fc8
17	♖ae1	*(10)*

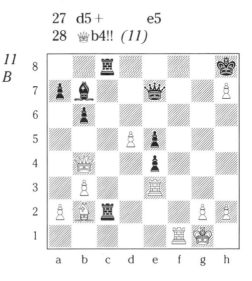

The final preparation for a central advance. This will clearly be decisive and only Blackburne's creative defence forces Zukertort to play so very magnificently in order to exploit his advantage.

17	...	♖c7
18	e4	♖ac8
19	e5	♘e8
20	f4	g6
21	♖e3	

Black is now forced to weaken his King's side, but in compensation he is able to achieve his objective on the 'c' file.

21	...	f5
22	ef	♘xf6
23	f5	♘e4

Obviously forced.

| 24 | ♗xe4 | de |
| 25 | fg!! | |

The beginning of a beautiful and deeply calculated combination.

| 25 | ... | ♖c2 |
| 26 | gh+ | ♚h8 |

Again Black's move is clearly forced as 26 ... ♚xh7 loses to 27 ♖h3+.

| 27 | d5+ | e5 |
| 28 | ♕b4!! | *(11)* |

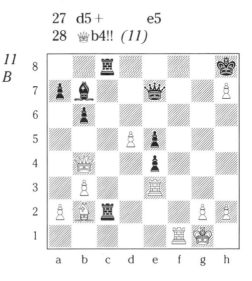

Blackburne wrote: 'An enthusiastic critic, who, by the by, was not present, says this literally electrified the lookers-on; whether this be so or not, at all events it was anticipated by me as there was no other move to save him from immediate loss. If the queen be taken White has a mate in seven moves.'

28 ...   ♖8c5

Forced, since if 28 ... ♕xb4 29 ♗xe5+ ♚xh7 30 ♖h3+ ♚g6 31 ♖g3+ ♚h7 32 ♖f7+ ♚h6 33 ♗f4+ ♚h5 34 ♖h7 mate.

Blackburne: 'I thought this sufficient, quite overlooking the sacrifice of the rook. At this stage walking round to see how the other games were going, one of the players said to me, "You've got the little man". "I don't know", I replied: "It's extremely difficult". On returning, Zukertort had not yet made his move, but it dawned on me that the sacrifice of the rook was fatal and the only question was whether he would find it out. This did not long remain doubtful. Returning to the other boards I presently heard a crash as though a piece were being slapped down with all the emphasis a man's muscles could give it, and presently there came a tap to my shoulder. "Your clock is going, I have made my move", he said, and from the expression of his face and the manner in which he drew himself up to his full height I felt that I might remark as the writer did when the audience damned his play, "He has found it out, has he?" '.

29   ♖f8+   ♚h7

Black cannot take the Rook. After 29 ... ♕xf8 30 ♗xe5+ ♚xh7 31 ♕xe4+ White soon mates.

30   ♕xe4+   ♚g7
31   ♗xe5+   ♚xf8
32   ♗g7+

Black resigned. Steinitz: 'One of the most noble combinations conceived over the chessboard and a worthy finish to one of the most brilliant games on record'.

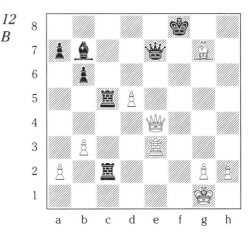

12 B

Flank Openings: 1 c4 and 1 ♘f3

1 c4 (Diagram 13). This opening move was mentioned by Lucena and by Ruy Lopez, the latter adding the comment that it is so bad that no

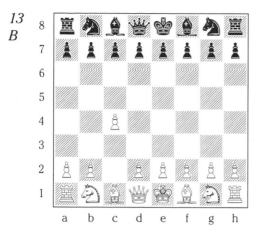

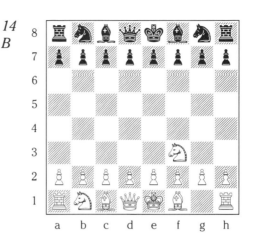

player of any skill would adopt it. Lopez was wrong! The modern history of the opening, and its name, both derive from the use of 1 c4 by Staunton in his 1843 match against Saint-Amant in Paris. Nowadays, the move 1 c4 is normally linked with the fianchetto, or flank development, of White's king's bishop to the g2 square. Strategically sharp positions result, in which White contests the central light squares in vigorous fashion. Those who have championed the English Opening include Staunton (of course), Réti, Nimzowitsch, Golombek, Botvinnik, Petrosian and, most recently, Kasparov, who added it to his repertoire for the 1987 World Championship match in Seville.

1 ♘f3 (Diagram 14). Although this move had reputedly been played by Napoleon, such games are generally deemed to be apochryphal. Zukertort used the move in the 19th century, but mainly as a method of transposing to a kind of delayed Queen's Gambit. It was only the contribution of the hypermodern Grandmaster Richard Réti (28 May 1889–6 June 1929) during the 1920s which welded 1 ♘f3 into a distinct system.

Réti demonstrated that 1 ♘f3 could lead into some of the most subtle and sophisticated positions on the chessboard. He held back his central pawns, while exerting pressure on the opponent's camp from fianchettoed long-range bishops operating from bases on b2 and g2. In 1924 at New York, Réti created a sensation, defeating none other than Capablanca with his new opening. This was the first game Capablanca had lost for eight years. Capablanca himself immediately became a convert to the opening. Others who followed in his path were Botvinnik, Smyslov and Petrosian.

4

A Champagne Victory

Steinitz–Tchigorin (Havana 1892)

T HE FIRST MAN to become official World Chess Champion was Wilhelm Steinitz, who held the title from 1886–94. Born in Prague, he moved to Vienna, where he tried to make a living as a journalist. The lure of chess, however, proved too strong and he eventually became a chess professional. In his first international tournament, played in London in 1862, he represented Austria. He subsequently decided to make his home in London, which was rapidly becoming the capital of world chess. Great tournaments were frequently held there after Staunton's pioneering efforts in staging the London 1851 experiment. Moreover chess centres, such as Simpson's Divan, were renowned as meeting places for the world's leading players. Simpson's, the most famous of these centres, was a natural extension of the chess playing coffee houses of the 18th century. It was known as a 'chess and cigar divan', and there amateurs could challenge the great masters for a stake, matches and tournaments were held and the enthusiast could catch up on the latest games and publications. Indeed, as we have seen, the Immortal Game, between Anderssen and Kieseritsky, was played in Simpson's as a casual game in 1851. It, and others like it, very much resembled a chess version of the celebrated London Gentlemen's clubs.

In terms of social history this was not the sort of milieu which would attract female players; moreover, despite the example of a queen regnant, women were heavily discouraged from entering male professions throughout the Victorian era. We should look to the historical development of a professional body of male chess players in the mid to late 19th century for a partial explanation, at the very least, of why women have seemingly been held back as exponents of the chess playing art.

Steinitz, although a foreigner, had no such disadvantages in the London chess scene of his time, and he rapidly became a denizen of Simpson's, where challenges from amateurs helped to augment his income. Once in London, Steinitz dominated British chess. In 1866 he won a match against Anderssen, the victor of London 1851, and he then went on to crush Bird and Blackburne, two of the leading English masters, in set contests. In 1872 Amos Burn recognised Steinitz as 'now probably the strongest living player'. *The Field* magazine invited Steinitz to contribute regular columns from 1873 to 1882 and he wrote for *Figaro* during the same period. His main journalistic effort was as proprietor and editor of the *International Chess Magazine* from 1885–91, a controversial and distinguished publication that is now a collector's item.

In the 1880s Johannes Zukertort emerged to challenge Steinitz's dominance. A fierce rivalry developed between the two men after Zukertort won the 1883 London tournament ahead of Steinitz and both men claimed to be the world's strongest player. In 1886 the issue was settled in the first World Championship Match in America, won overwhelmingly by Steinitz. The demoralized Zukertort was now broken in health and died two years later. Steinitz succeeded in sweeping aside challenges from Tchigorin and Gunsberg, but in 1894 suffered painful defeat at the hands of the youthful Emanuel Lasker, who at the age of 25 wrested the World Championship from his veteran opponent. A return match was held in Moscow two years later, but it would have been better for Steinitz if he had never played. He lost 10 games, drew 5 and won 2. This stinging humiliation caused a mental breakdown and he insisted he could make telephone calls without the need for any apparatus. Steinitz was briefly interned in the Moscow Morossov asylum. The full account of his brutal maltreatment can be read in Ludwig Bachmann's book *Schachmeister Steinitz*. Mercifully he recovered and was at Morossov for a month before his release. For some years Steinitz continued to play successfully in tournaments, but in 1900 he died in utter poverty in New York and was given a pauper's burial at the Evergreen Cemetery, Brooklyn. The memory of his final destitution has haunted masters of the game ever since and had bitter echoes in the death of Alexander Alekhine, the fourth man to hold the world title.

Steinitz, however, left a legacy of profound influence on the strategic development of the game. He displayed a deep understanding of defensive play, which included the accumulation of small advantages, and the creation of weaknesses for the opponent, such as isolated and doubled pawns. His ideas were published in his book *Modern Chess Theory* in 1889. His consummate grasp of strategy is demonstrated in the following game from his World Championship match against Tchigorin played in Havana in 1892, three years before the second Cuban rebellion against Spain for Independence.

Mikhail Tchigorin

Wilhelm Steinitz

Tchigorin was born near St Petersburg in 1850, where he later founded a chess club. Although he worked for a while as a government official, he developed a devotion to chess in his mid-twenties and gave up his post in order to pursue the life of a chess professional. In 1883 he was placed fourth in the great London tournament and in 1889 he first unsuccessfully challenged Steinitz for the World Championship. His best tournament results were achieved in the 1890s, including second place at Hastings 1895.

The following game was a vitally important clash in the series of World Championship Matches between the Austrian and Russian champions. The game was notable for the bracing refreshments selected by the masters during play. Tchigorin was supplied with free brandy and Steinitz with unlimited champagne. Their glasses stood beside the board during play. Steinitz explained later that he drank the champagne under medical advice in order to fortify his nerves.

White: Steinitz
Black: Tchigorin
World Championship, 4th match game, Havana 1892
RUY LOPEZ

1	e4	e5
2	♘f3	♘c6
3	♗b5	♘f6
4	d3	

The fashionable move now is 4 0-0 but there is nothing wrong with this quiet reinforcement of the centre and 4 ♕e2 (as suggested by Ruy Lopez himself) is also playable.

4	...	d6
5	c3	g6
6	♘bd2	♗g7
7	♘f1	0-0
8	♗a4	♘d7 *(15)*

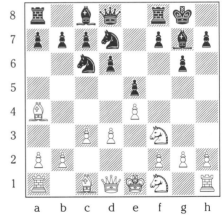

15 W

Tchigorin seems to be organizing the break ... f5, but this plan is faulty. He should either have left the king's knight at its post and gone for immediate queenside expansion (8 ... a6 9 ♘e3 b5 10 ♗b3 ♘a5 11 ♗c2 c5) or else he should have met 9 ♘e3 with ... ♘b6, trying to get in ... d5.

9	♘e3	♘c5
10	♗c2	♘e6
11	h4	♘e7

| 12 | h5 | d5 |
| 13 | hxg6 | fxg6? |

A severe positional error ('always capture towards the centre' is one of the better 'rules') in that Black irretrievably weakens the diagonal on which the king is situated. After 13 ... hxg6 White had nothing immediate.

14	ed	♘xd5
15	♘xd5	♕xd5
16	♗b3	♕c6 *(16)*

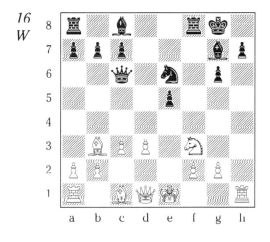

16 W

White controls two powerful open lines towards the black king and, in view of Tchigorin's lack of counterplay, it only remains for Steinitz to mobilize the remainder of his forces before the decisive attack inevitably materializes.

17	♕e2	♗d7
18	♗e3	♔h8
19	0-0-0	♖ae8
20	♕f1	

A very fine move which prepares to open two new avenues of attack.

| 20 | ... | a5 |

The wretched situation of Black's king leaves him curiously helpless to defend against the coming onslaught.

21	d4	exd4
22	♘xd4	♗xd4
23	♖xd4!	

There are so many threats at this point (even the simple ♖4h4 will be deadly) that Black may as well grab the exchange.

| 23 | ... | ♘xd4 |
| 24 | ♖xh7+!! *(17)* | |

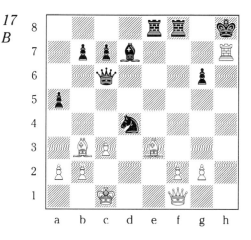

17 B

A beautiful denouement. Just as everyone was waiting for execution along the twin diagonals, Steinitz reveals his true plans with this stunning surprise.

| 24 | ... | ♔xh7 |
| 25 | ♕h1+ | |

A most original point of departure for a mating attack along the h–file.

25	...	♚ g7
26	♗ h6+	♚ f6
27	♛ h4+	♚ e5
28	♛ xd4+	♚ f5
29	♛ f4 *(18)*	

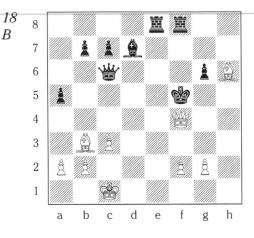

18 B

Checkmate.

Ruy Lopez

Ruy Lopez was a 16th century Spanish Priest, a favourite at the Court of King Philip II. In 1561 Lopez published a book of chess openings and general precepts, which included the suggestion that the board be placed so that the sun shines in the eyes of your opponent. The opening moves of the Ruy Lopez (or Spanish) opening are: 1 e4 e5 2 ♘f3 ♘c6 3 ♗b5 (Diagram 19). At this point Black has a wide variety of defences against White's strategy of exerting pressure against the pawn on e5. The Lopez is considered one of the most sophisticated openings and has been a favourite of Steinitz, Capablanca, Fischer and Karpov.

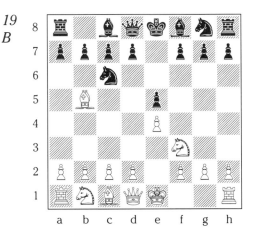

19 B

5

BATTLE OF TITANS

Pillsbury–Lasker (St Petersburg 1896)

E MANUEL LASKER held the World Championship title for a record 27 years from 1894 to 1921. No one has ever equalled this achievement. Not only did he defend the title regularly against powerful opposition, he also won nearly every tournament that he entered during his long reign. Even after he lost the title he continued to notch up first class tournament victories and was still competing successfully at the age of 67.

Lasker's play always fascinated the public, as he overcame outstanding Grandmasters in droves. Some even accused him of hypnotising or bewitching his hapless opponents. In reality he was one of the first players to apply psychology to the chessboard, deploying moves which may not have been the strongest, but which he felt were unpleasant for an individual opponent. He was the perfect fighter, rejoicing in the struggle for its own sake, unafraid of risks and possessed of amazingly intricate understanding of the game. His special skills centred on the middlegame, where he created incredible complications. If his adversaries survived these, then they were remorselessly ground down in the endgame. If chess is, as I maintain, a mirror of intellectual developments in other spheres, it is fascinating to observe that Lasker's reliance on psychological warfare, probing the weaknesses of his opponents' chessboard psyche, was developed at approximately the same time that Sigmund Freud was analysing the subconscious mind in Vienna.

Lasker was born in Prussia in 1868 and established his reputation in tournaments and match play in Germany, England and the United States in a burst of activity from 1889 to 1893. His astounding breakthrough came in the World Championship match of 1894 against the old war horse Steinitz. At the outset Lasker, aged 25, was regarded as an inexperienced contender, but his mastery developed as the match progressed. He took the title with ten wins, 4 draws and 5 losses.

The following year Lasker played in the inaugural Hastings tournament, the strongest chess competition ever held up to that time. With three rounds to go the youthful World Champion led the field, which included Steinitz and Tchigorin. Lasker was, however, recuperating from a severe case of typhoid fever and was overtaken by Harry Pillsbury, the American who was making his first appearance on the international circuit. No one had ever won such an event at their first attempt. The fact that Lasker could only come in third place at Hastings encouraged his successful rivals

Harry Pillsbury

Pillsbury and Tchigorin to believe that they could demonstrate their superiority even more clearly over a man who was beginning to look like a stop-gap champion.

Accordingly, Tchigorin invited the winners from Hastings to participate in a multi-round tournament in St Petersburg, the cultural capital of Tsarist Russia. Pillsbury and Tchigorin were regarded as the likely victors, because Steinitz was nearing 60 and Lasker was erroneously believed to be too frail. At the half-way stage Pillsbury was a point clear of the field, but around this time it is believed that he discovered that he had contracted syphilis and his morale collapsed. Lasker played in brilliant form to take the victory in this event, thus confirming his right to the World Championship.

After St Petersburg, Lasker continued to notch up a sensational series of firsts: in Nuremburg that same year, in London 1899 and Paris 1900. Perhaps he now found chess too simple and withdrew temporarily from active play to the study of mathematics and philosophy, but in 1908 he returned to the fray, defending his world title against in turn Tarrasch, Schlechter, Marshall and Janowsky, a string of formidable opponents. His last great tournament win as champion came when he returned to St Petersburg in 1914. The Great War of 1914–18 served to undermine Lasker's financial resources and his health and in 1921 he lost the title to the young Cuban star Capablanca in a match held in Havana. Sadly, Lasker failed to win a single game in this, his last championship appearance.

Nevertheless, he continued to best his younger rivals in tournament play, including taking first prize at New York in 1924 ahead of both Capablanca and the Russian Alekhine. It was here that he demonstrated that in certain circumstances a lone knight can draw against the opponent's rook and pawn, an amazingly complex discovery.

The advent of the Nazis in Germany forced Lasker, a Jew by birth, into exile, and he travelled the tournament circuit once again in order to make a living. His results were still outstanding. He died in New York in 1941.

The game that I have chosen to illustrate Lasker's unique talents was played in the tenth round at St Petersburg 1896. This was the true test. Lasker faced the victor of Hastings 1895, and had to prove that he, and not Pillsbury, was the real World Champion.

His opponent, Pillsbury, was capable of astonishing feats of mental exertion. One of his specialities was to play 12 games of chess, 6 games of draughts and a hand of duplicate whist simultaneously. He would also memorize a series of thirty incredibly obscure words, then write them out and repeat them verbally in sequence, first forwards and then backwards. The list included words such as 'antiphlogistine', 'staphylococcus' and 'salmagundi'. All this must have represented a considerable strain on his brain. In 1904, at Cambridge Springs, Pillsbury achieved the worst tournament result of his life. In the following year he tried to kill himself by jumping from the fourth floor of the Philadelphia Presbyterian Hospital, during, as the local *Evening Bulletin* recorded 'a period of temporary insanity'. He was subdued by staff at the hospital, but by 1906, at the tragically early age of 34, he was dead.

White: Pillsbury
Black: Lasker
St Petersburg 1896
QUEEN'S GAMBIT DECLINED

This famous game has been hailed as a superhuman effort, containing a combination described as 'one of the greatest feats of the human imagination'. This was the true test. There had been much talk about Lasker's right to the World Championship. In spite of his victory (1894) over Steinitz he had already suffered two defeats by Pillsbury in the present Battle of Titans. This was the crucial game. If Lasker did not win, he was unlikely to catch Pillsbury and confirm his right to the world title. Lasker the fighter rose to the occasion and entered a struggle to the death. Suffice it to say that after this defeat Pillsbury – usually a calm and unruffled individual – lost the next four games in a row, thus not only forfeiting first place but ending up third behind Steinitz. This is one of the greatest games in our vast chess literature.

1   d4

Pillsbury also realizes the tenseness of the situation and tries the weapon with which he had so much success at Hastings, the tournament Pillsbury had just won, ahead of Lasker!

1	...	d5
2	c4	e6
3	♘c3	♘f6
4	♘f3	c5
5	♗g5	cxd4
6	♕xd4	♘c6

Safer is 6 ... ♗e7, but Lasker was not seeking safety.

7   ♕h4

Sharper is 7 ♗xf6 gf 8 ♕h4.

7	...	♗e7
8	0-0-0	♕a5
9	e3	♗d7
10	♔b1	h6!
11	cxd5	exd5
12	♘d4	0-0
13	♗xf6	♗xf6
14	♕h5	♘xd4
15	exd4	♗e6
16	f4?	*(20)*

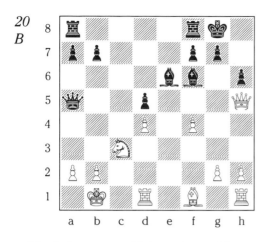

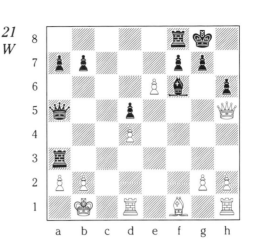

Much better would have been 16 ♗d3 ♖xd4 17 ♗h7+ ♚xh7 18 ♖xd4 and the d-pawn must fall. But one cannot criticise Pillsbury for underestimating Black's counterchances.

16	...	♖ac8
17	f5	

Here 17 ♕f3 was essential.

17	...	♖xc3!
18	fxe6	

With 18 bxc3 ♕xc3 19 ♕f3 ♕b4+ 20 ♕b3 ♗xf5+ 21 ♗d3 ♕xb3+ 22 axb3 ♗g4 23 ♖c1 ♗xd4 24 ♖c7 ♖e8 25 ♖f1 ♖e3 Pillsbury could have put up a battle, though probably a losing one. The text, however, seems much safer.

18	...	♖a3!! *(21)*

A problem-like move.

19 exf7+

If 19 bxa3 ♕b6+ 20 ♚a1 ♗xd4+ 21 ♖xd4 ♕xd4+ 22 ♚b1 fxe6 followed by 23 ... ♖f2 winning. A variation similar to this explains White's 21st move. On the other hand, if 19 e7 ♖e8 20 bxa3 ♕b6+ 21 ♚c2 ♖c8+ 22 ♚d2 ♗xd4 23 e8(=♕)+ ♖xe8 24 ♗d3 ♕a5+ 25 ♚c1 ♕xa3+!

19	...	♖xf7
20	bxa3	♕b6+
21	♗b5	

See the previous note.

21	...	♕xb5+
22	♚a1	♖c7!

If 22 ... ♕c4 then 23 ♕g4 holds.

23	♖d2	♖c4
24	♖hd1	

If 24 ♖b1 ♕c5.

24	...	♜c3
25	♛f5	♛c4
26	♚b2?	

Both players were now pressed for time and here Pillsbury misses the fine defensive move 26 ♛b1. After 26 ... ♜xa3 27 ♛b2 Black will have a difficult time working out a win.

26	...	♜xa3! *(22)*

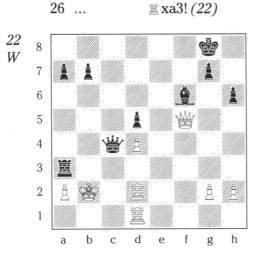

Another problem move.

27	♛e6+	♚h7
28	♚xa3	

If 28 ♚b1 ♝xd4 29 ♛f5+ g6 30 ♛f7+ ♝g7 31 ♛xb7 ♜a4 32 ♜b2 ♛e4+ winning. Black now mates in five moves.

28	...	♛c3+
29	♚a4	b5+
30	♚xb5	♛c4+
31	♚a5	♝d8+
32	♛b6	axb6 *(23)*

Checkmate. A colossal struggle.

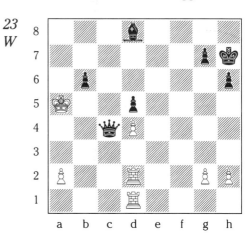

The Queen's Gambit

This opening, 1 d4 d5 2 c4 (Diagram 24), first became popular in the mid-18th century, as a result of games by Philip Stamma. Stamma was a native of Aleppo in Syria and, according to Harry Golombek, a belated representative of the great Arab School of Chess. In 1745 he published *The Noble Game of Chess* in which he strongly advocated use of the Queen's Gambit. Not surprisingly, this opening originally became known as 'The Gambit of Aleppo'.

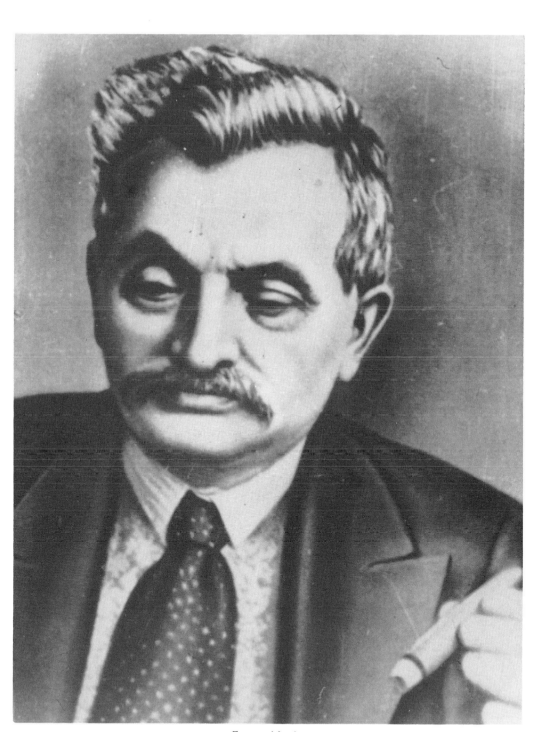

Emanuel Lasker

24
B

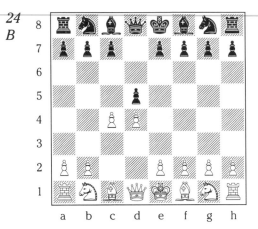

Lord Harrington, Stamma's patron in London, helped secure him the appointment of Interpreteur of Oriental Languages by Royal Warrant, dated 14th August 1739 and signed by King George II. This post earned him a salary of £80 per annum. In 1747 in Slaughter's Coffee House in Saint Martin's Lane, London, Stamma was beaten by 8 losses with 1 win and 1 draw by the rising star Philidor. Nevertheless, Stamma's Gambit has survived to become the subtle Queen's side equivalent of the Ruy Lopez. It has been a favourite of Lasker, Alekhine, Botvinnik and Kasparov.

6

■ ▫ ■ ▫ ■ ▫ ■ ▫ ■ ▫ ■ ▫ ■ ▫ ■ ▫ ■ ▫ ■ ▫ ■ ▫ ■ ▫ ■ ▫ ■ ▫ ■ ▫ ■ ▫ ■ ▫ ■ ▫ ■ ▫ ■ ▫

THE THUNDERBOLT

Bernstein–Capablanca (Moscow 1914)

C APABLANCA was the greatest player that the Caribbean islands have ever produced. He was born in Havana in 1888 and learnt chess at the age of four, amazingly with no formal tuition. Instead, he picked up the moves by watching his father play with friends. This was just about the time when the World Championship match between Steinitz and Tchigorin was being played in Capablanca's home town, where chess was headline news.

The Cuban was the first modern chessplayer to achieve superstar status. His name was known to millions throughout the world, even those who did not play chess. Only Morphy, Fischer and Kasparov have achieved similar widespread renown. In his 1921 match, when he toppled Lasker from the world throne, he became the only man in the history of chess not to lose a single game whilst winning the World Championship. The myth of invincibility clung to him throughout his career and there was universal shock when he lost the coveted title in 1927 to the Russian, Alekhine, after a mammoth struggle involving an amazing 25 draws.

Capablanca's education was sponsored by a local industrialist, who paid for his protegé's schooling in America. In 1906 he went to Columbia University to study engineering, but spent most of his time at the famed Manhattan Chess Club, where he played frequently against Lasker, the then World Champion. In 1908 his patron withdrew his support and Capablanca was left to try to earn his living as a chess player. At first his earnings were thin, but in the following year he defeated Frank Marshall in a decisive match, winning 8 games, losing one and drawing 14. At Marshall's generous insistence the young Cuban was invited to play in the tournament of San Sebastian in

1911. This was intended to be an elite event, where all the contestants were supposed to have won at least one Grandmaster tournament. Two other participants, Nimzowitsch and Bernstein protested that Capablanca should not be included. Honour demanded that Capablanca should destroy his antagonists and carry off first prize, both of which he did.

Two years later the Cuban government rewarded Capablanca with a position in the Foreign Office which afforded him ample opportunity for travelling and playing chess. He had no particular duties, but was to be an international ambassador, a famous and attractive figure, representing Cuba wherever he went. In 1921 he crowned his chess career by winning the world title from Lasker in his home city, Havana.

During the 1920s, however, his tournament record as World Champion was neither very active nor overly imposing. His fortunes seemed to revive in New York in 1927, when he won an immensely strong, six player, quadruple round, tournament without losing a single game over 20 rounds. Once again the myth of invincibility was

Capablanca and Lasker

revived. Yet a few months later, just ten days before his 39th birthday, Capablanca conceded defeat in his world title match against Alekhine. Writing much later Alekhine explained that Capablanca had made the fatal error of overestimating his own powers and underestimating those of his opponent.

Capablanca never raised the prize stakes necessary for a return match, although he continued to play in tournaments with mixed results. In 1936 he won a powerful tournament in Moscow a point ahead of Botvinnik. In the same year he tied with Botvinnik for first place at the Category 14 Nottingham tournament, ahead of the then World Champion, Max Euwe. His last first-class games were played in the 1939 Olympiad in Buenos Aires, where he played first board for Cuba. The outbreak of the Second World War whilst the Olympiad was in progress heralded a period of disruption for many of the world's leading players. Capablanca was not to play at top level again and he died of a heart attack in the Manhattan Chess Club in 1942.

In Cuba, Capablanca has left a legacy of fervour for chess. Since the 1959 revolution chess has been given extensive official encouragement. In 1966 Havana was host to the 17th chess Olympiad, when Fidel Castro played chess with both Bobby Fischer and Tigran Petrosian.

The game I have chosen to display Capablanca's great classical style was played against his one-time detractor from San Sebastian 1911, the Ukranian-born lawyer Ossip Bernstein. On this occasion they were facing each other in Moscow in 1914. Bernstein's career illustrates the disastrous effects that the two World Wars had for many chess players. He lost his fortune during the 1917 Russian Revolution and like so many exiles settled in Paris. He was driven from his successful legal practice in the French capital in 1940, when the Germans took Paris. He fled to Spain, returning to France only after the war had finished, and was still playing fine chess at international level well into his seventies.

White: Bernstein
Black: Capablanca
Moscow 1914
QUEEN'S GAMBIT DECLINED

1	d4	d5
2	c4	e6

If Black accepts the pawn with 2 ... dxc4 White has several ways to regain the material. One possibility is

3 ♕a4+ and ♕xc4. In that case Black would have abandoned his foothold in the centre.

3	♘f3	♘f6
4	♘c3	♗e7
5	♗g5	0-0
6	e3	♘bd7
7	♖c1	b6
8	cxd5	exd5

Bern 1932: Bogolyubov stands at the front with Bernstein directly behind and Alekhine and Flohr in the foreground to his left.

Capablanca was perfectly happy to play the Queen's Gambit both with White and with Black. In the famous Capablanca–Alekhine match of 1927, no fewer than 32 games from the 34 total were Queen's Gambits.

9	♕a4

A more active move is 9 ♗b5.

9	..	♗b7 *(25)*

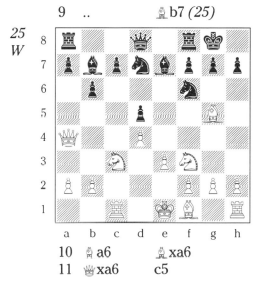

10	♗a6	♗xa6
11	♕xa6	c5

With this move Black announces that he has freed his game.

12	♗xf6	♘xf6
13	dxc5	bxc5
14	0-0	♕b6
15	♕e2	c4
16	♖fd1	

White's strategy is to bombard Black's two central pawns on the d- and c-files. Nevertheless, an irony of this game is that White's eventual success in winning one of these pawns is what brings about his downfall.

16	...	♖fd8 *(26)*

17	♘d4	♗b4
18	b3	♖ac8
19	bxc4	dxc4
20	♖c2	♗xc3
21	♖xc3	♘d5

Black has just one pawn left in the centre, the passed pawn on c4. The question is, is this pawn strong or weak? Obviously, Bernstein cannot capture it immediately since 22 ♖xc4 allows ... ♘c3 and Black wins rook for knight.

22	♖c2	c3
23	♖dc1	♖c5

Now, at long last, White sets in motion a manoeuvre which wins the bold black pawn which has advanced so far into the White camp.

24	♘b3	♖c6
25	♘d4	♖c7
26	♘b5	♖c5 *(27)*

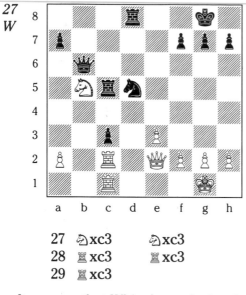

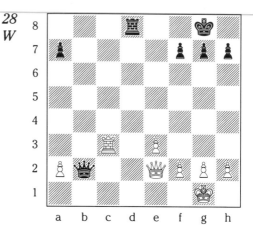

27 ♘xc3   ♘xc3
28 ♖xc3   ♖xc3
29 ♖xc3

It appears that White has calculated well, for 29 ... ♕b1+ 30 ♕f1 ♖d1 fails to 31 ♖d8 mate. However, what else can Black do to make up for his lost pawn? The answer is swift in coming.

29 ...   ♕b2!! *(28)*

White has no choice, faced by this thunderbolt, but to resign. The variations, in which Capablanca forces a win with mathematical precision, are fascinating:

(1) 30 ♕xb2 ♖d1 checkmate;

(2) 30 ♖c8 ♕a1+ 31 ♕f1 ♕xf1+ 32 ♔xf1 ♖xc8 with an extra rook;

(3) 30 ♖c2 ♕b1+ 31 ♕f1 ♕xc2 also winning a rook;

(4) 30 ♕e1 ♕xc3 31 ♕xc3 ♖d1+ 32 ♕e1 ♖xe1 checkmate.

7

THE MARSHAL'S BATON

Bogolyubov–Alekhine (Hastings 1922)

T HE STORY OF Alexander Alekhine's life is a mixture of powerful artistry and tragically misdirected genius. A political trimmer, he supported whatever regime would allow him to earn a living as a chess player. The nadir came in 1941 when he published three articles in the Nazi press directed against Jewish players. His subsequent denial of authorship was disproved in 1956 when the holograph manuscripts were found amongst his wife's effects.

Moreover, a predilection for alcohol and the turn of historical fate combined to produce one of the most turbulent careers in the history of chess. Alekhine was born in Moscow in 1892 of a family that was both wealthy and aristocratic. He and his brother were taught chess by their mother and in 1909 he gained the master title in St Petersburg.

Alekhine was playing in Mannheim at the outbreak of the war in 1914, when he was interned by the Germans, his release doubtless obtained by family influence. In 1915 he joined the Russian Red Cross and served on the Austrian front. The Revolution of 1917 destroyed the family fortune and he worked as a magistrate and chess player, winning the first Soviet Championship in 1920. He joined the Communist Party in 1921 and worked as an official interpreter, but later settled in France as a naturalized citizen. From the safety of exile he attacked the Soviet regime. His later attempts to conciliate with the Soviet authorities failed and he never returned to Russia, where the Communist regime was giving increasing prominence and support to chess and its foremost exponents.

From 1921 to 1927 our anti-hero ran up a string of tournament victories, but his

Efim Bogolyubov

ultimate goal was to take the world title from Capablanca. In 1927 the Cuban accepted Alekhine's challenge, and unexpectedly conceded the title after a mammoth struggle in Buenos Aires. Although he now dominated the chess world like a Colossus, brushing aside the resistance of established Grandmasters as if they were mere beginners, discerning critics noticed disturbing signs of impatience in Alekhine's games. Not content with the inevitable incidence of drawn games, when one is facing strong opposition, Alekhine began to force events at every turn, running hideous risks in his desperate efforts to crush every opponent.

By 1935 Alekhine's impatience had become compounded by a new reliance on the stimulation offered by alcohol. More or less in a perpetual stupor he lost his title in 1935 to the Dutchman, Max Euwe. The pre-match contract had stipulated that Alekhine had the right to a return bout. Alarmed by his loss, Alekhine suppressed his desire for drink and regained the title from Euwe in 1937, thus becoming the first man to win the World Championship twice. He retained the title until his death, the only man ever to die while in possession of the world title.

He was playing for France in the Buenos Aires Olympiad of 1939 when war was declared and as captain he refused to allow his team to play against Germany. On returning to Europe he joined the French army as an interpreter and fled to Lisbon, where displaced European aristocrats and other exiles took up residence during the war. In 1941 he fell under Nazi influence. Not ony did the regrettable articles appear in print, perhaps losing him the chance of a visa to the USA, but he also played in tournaments in Germany and in occupied countries. After the war, these actions were later construed as collaboration and in 1946 he was refused an invitation to the London tournament. He was also suffering from the effects of years of hard drinking.

Alekhine was, of course, still World Champion – the opportunity for matches having been severely limited by the constraints of world war, and the young challenger Mikhail Botvinnik was eager for a match to take place. This was arranged in March 1946 under the auspices of the British Chess Federation, but the day after the news was despatched by telegram Alekhine died from a heart attack. Alekhine would have undoubtedly lost had he played Botvinnik, but the match would have done much to restore his fortunes and reputation.

The game I have chosen comes from Hastings 1922, and was considered by many experts to be the most brilliant game of chess ever played. The significance of this game was that it came as one of the first mighty clashes between two Russian Grandmasters who in the later 1920s and early 1930s were to contend two series of world title matches against each other. Alekhine's opponent Bogolyubov was the only man ever to hold the German and Soviet Championships at the same time.

Bogolyubov defected from the USSR in 1926 and was declared a traitor, his name only being rehabilitated in 1977, 25 years after his death. Bogolyubov was a portly figure, an eternal optimist and a child of nature, possessed of a river of flowing ideas, when in action on the chess board. His poetic skills in that medium were not matched by his appearance. At one tournament the official photographer cut Bogolyubov in fact the senior Grandmaster present, out of the picture since he thought that a rotund gentleman brandishing a glass of beer had no place in a record of chess masters.

White: Bogolyubov
Black: Alekhine
Hastings 1922
DUTCH DEFENCE

1	d4	f5
2	c4	♘f6
3	g3	e6
4	♗g2	♗b4+

The Dutch Defence is often considered risky, but Alekhine, as in this case, resorted to it when he absolutely had to win with Black. The point is, that the early move of Black's f-pawn slightly weakens Black's king's field. On the other hand, if Black survives the opening, then the aggressive move of the f-pawn will grant him greater influence over the centre. It should also be noted, that in the 19th century, when chess science was in its infancy, the advantage of playing with the white pieces was not so marked. As the 20th century advanced and investigation into chess openings became more intensive, the initiative conferred by playing White began to take on a similar edge to having the advantage of the serve in tennis.

5	♗d2	♗xd2+
6	♘xd2	

Passive. White should retake with the queen.

6	...	♘c6
7	♘gf3	0-0
8	0-0	d6
9	♕b3	♔h8

Black's king moves out of the diagonal of the white queen: a useful precaution.

10	♕c3	

Passive again. White should strike out with 10 d5.

10	...	e5

This move looks as if it loses a pawn, but if 11 dxe5 dxe5 12 ♘xe5 ♘xe5 13 ♕xe5 ♕xd2 and suddenly Black has won a knight.

11	e3	a5
12	b3	♕e8

Black's queen travels to h5 where it joins in an attack against the white king.

Alexander Alekhine

13 a3   ♛h5
14 h4

Again White is unable to win a pawn; viz: 14 dxe5 dxe5 15 ♘xe5 ♘xe5 16 ♛xe5 ♘g4 with a double attack against White's queen and the pawn on h2. The latter is particularly significant since the threat would be ... ♛xh2 checkmate. Such cunning tactical points abound in Alekhine's games.

14 ...   ♘g4 *(29)*

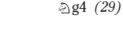

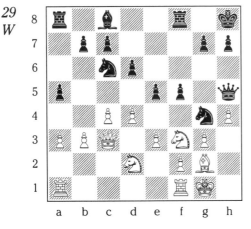

Now that White has been obliged to advance his h-pawn to avoid Black's threats in that sector, Black's knight can assume a powerful and secure post on g4. White's attempts to dislodge it only result in further pawn weaknesses.

15 ♘g5   ♗d7
16 f3   ♘f6
17 f4   e4
18 ♖fd1   h6
19 ♘h3   d5
20 ♘f1   ♘e7
21 a4   ♘c6

The knight returns. There is now a hole on the b4 square which Black can utilize to invade the White position, ultimately advancing his knight via b4 to d3.

22 ♖d2   ♘b4
23 ♗h1   ♛e8
24 ♖g2   dxc4
25 bxc4   ♗xa4
26 ♘f2   ♗d7
27 ♘d2   b5
28 ♘d1   ♘d3

Black's manoeuvres have gained him a pawn. Nevertheless, it is extremely difficult to maintain this slight material advantage since White exerts serious pressure against the Black queen's flank. Alekhine now decides to surrender the extra pawn voluntarily. This is, though, merely the introduction to one of the grandest combinations ever conceived. Watch now as, over the next five moves, Black's pawn on b5 marches straight through the White position while White captures, in sequence, both of Black's rooks and the black queen, even giving check *en route*.

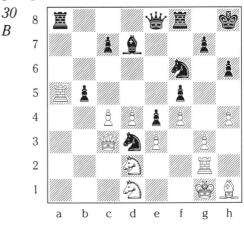

29 ♖xa5 *(30)* b4
30 ♖xa8 bxc3
31 ♖xe8 c2!!

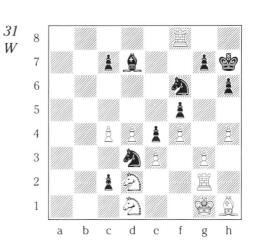

31
W

The point of the combination. Black also sacrifices the rook on f8 with check in order to ensure the promotion of his pawn.

32 ♖xf8+ ♚h7 *(31)*

New York 1924: Standing (left to right) Tartakower, Maroczy, Alekhine, Reti and Bogolyubov. Seated (left to right) Capablanca, Janowski, Ed. Lasker and Em. Lasker.

33	♘f2	c1 (= ♛) +	
34	♘f1		

After the mighty whirlwind of complications, the balance of forces on both sides is approximately equal. However, White's tangled knot of pieces around his king is no match for the mobile black queen.

34	...	♘e1

Threatening ... ♘f3 checkmate, a smothered mate to end all smothered mates.

35	♖h2	♛xc4
36	♖b8	♗b5

White now has no choice but to give up his rook for the dangerous black bishop. Gradually, material advantage shifts in Black's favour.

37	♖xb5	♛xb5
38	g4	♘f3 +
39	♗xf3	exf3
40	gxf5	♛e2
41	d5	♚g8
42	h5	♚h7
43	e4	♘xe4
44	♘xe4	♛xe4
45	d6	cxd6
46	f6	gxf6

47	♖d2	♛e2! (32)

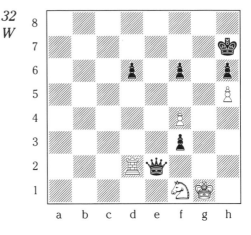

32
W

A fitting end to this wonderful game. Black adds a queen sacrifice to force a winning endgame of kings and pawns.

48	♖xe2	fxe2
49	♚f2	exf1 (= ♛) +
50	♚xf1	♚g7
51	♚f2	♚f7
52	♚e3	♚e6
53	♚e4	d5 +

White resigns. In order to stop the advance of Black's d-pawn, White will have to lose both of his pawns on the f- and h-files. Thus, 54 ♚d4 ♚f5 55 ♚xd5 ♚xf4 56 ♚e6 ♚g5 when White is helpless.

8

■ ■

PARALYSIS

Sämisch–Nimzowitsch (Copenhagen 1923)

T HE LATVIAN-JEWISH Grandmaster, Aron Nimzowitsch, was the leading exponent of the Hypermodern school, which held, amongst other tenets, that control of the centre of the board can be achieved without occupation by pawns. He belongs to a small group of players who for one reason or another were denied at the peak of their powers the opportunity to challenge for the world title. In the late 1920s and early 1930s he was overshadowed even at the height of his career by Capablanca and Alekhine. In retaliation he pompously and self-consciously adopted the title 'crown prince of the chess world'.

At the age of 8 Nimzowitsch was taught chess by his father. He later recorded in a brief autobiography how his father had 'demonstrated to me Anderssen's Immortal Game', which had a profound effect – 'I not only understood it, but at once fell passionately in love with it'. It was not until 1904, whilst studying mathematics in Germany, that Nimzowitsch began to concentrate on chess play. His most notable successes came after the mid-1920s, when he won at Marienbad in 1925 (with Rubinstein), and took outright victory at Dresden and Hannover in 1926. A brilliant first place at Carlsbad 1929 was achieved ahead of Capablanca, Euwe and Bogolyubov.

Ill health caused a sudden decline in Nimzowitsch's play in the 1930s. He was taken fatally sick at the end of 1934 and died of pneumonia after a lingering illness of three months duration at the age of 48. His greatest contribution was to chess literature and theory. He is remembered as author of *My System*, perhaps the most influential chess book ever written, published in 1925 and as the pioneer of the Nimzo-Indian Defence.

Nimzowitsch's theories were a direct challenge to those of Dr Siegbert Tarrasch, leader of the classical school. The differences between the two men were more than theoretical. Nimzowitsch described his adversary as 'my born enemy' and declared 'Tarrasch to me always meant mediocrity; it is true that he was a very strong player, but all his views, his sympathies and antipathies, and above all his inability to conceive any new idea – all this clearly attested to the full mediocrity of his cast of mind'.

Aron Nimzowitsch

Perhaps Nimzowitsch's greatest talent lay in his ability to convey established chess practice by the elaboration of a new chess vocabulary. He introduced such phrases as 'hanging pawns', 'prophylaxis' and 'mysterious rook move', thus assisting clarity of thought and speed of comprehension for his readers.

Nimzowitsch also advocated the psychological concept of 'heroic defence' – the deliberate choice of complex positions, which would drag the opponent into a maelstrom where draws would be unlikely. This conscious appeal to raw struggle, in which established orthodoxies were challenged, had its parallel in other contemporary intellectual activities, it could be seen in Dada and Surrealism, in the seemingly impenetrable writings of Franz Kafka and in the wild rhythms of Stravinsky's 'Sacré du Printemps' that so scandalized its first audience.

The success of Nimzowitsch's theories can be gauged from his spectacular tournament results, and in the fact that since the 1920s *My System* has retained its appeal as the essential book on chess strategy.

The following game was played in Copenhagen 1923 against the German Grandmaster Friedrich Sämisch, who had the unwelcome distinction of losing more games on time than any other master. In 1969 in Linköping he lost all 13 of his games in this fashion. Paradoxically, he played speed chess well and in his 61st year won two lightning tournaments. Sämisch's team members, noting that the Grandmaster was addicted to tobacco, sought to eliminate his fatally long periods of thinking by stealing his pipe at regular intervals, only returning it when he had made his move.

White: Sämisch
Black: Nimzowitsch
Copenhagen 1923
QUEEN'S INDIAN DEFENCE

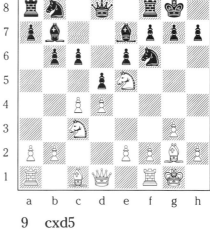

33
W

1	d4	♘f6
2	c4	e6
3	♘f3	b6
4	g3	♗b7
5	♗g2	♗e7
6	♘c3	0-0
7	0-0	d5
8	♘e5	c6 *(33)*
9	cxd5	

This move is a premature release of the tension which solves most of Black's problems. Much more vigorous is 9 e4, advancing boldly in the centre.

9	...	cxd5
10	♗f4	a6
11	♖c1	b5
12	♕b3	♘c6
13	♘xc6	

White eliminates the black knight since he is scared of the manoeuvre ... ♘c6–a5–c4.

13	...	♗xc6
14	h3	♕d7
15	♔h2	♘h5
16	♗d2	f5
17	♕d1	b4 *(34)*

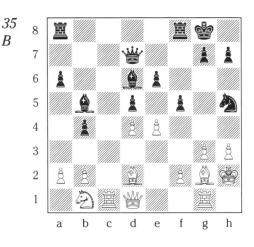

34 W

Black is gradually increasing his control of terrain on both sides of the board. At the moment, this amounts to a surreptitious square here and a stealthy diagonal there. Ultimately, however, it builds up to a case of megalomaniac world domination on the 64 squares.

18	♘b1	♗b5
19	♖g1	♗d6

With this move, it looks as if Nimzowitsch is falling into White's trap. It is, though, Black who has seen much further.

    20 e4 *(35)*

35 B

Sämisch must have breathed a sigh of relief when he made this freeing move. The point is that White's queen on d1 suddenly attacks the knight on h5. If Black now had to play 20 ... ♕f7 then 21 e5 ♗e7 22 f4 would completely consolidate the White fortress. But Nimzowitsch is ready with a brilliant sacrifice of his knight for two pawns.

20	...	fxe4!!
21	♕xh5	♖xf2
22	♕g5	♖af8
23	♔h1	♖8f5
24	♕e3	♗d3
25	♖ce1	h6 *(36)*

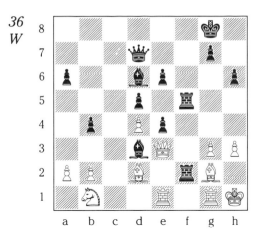

36 W

Friedrich Sämisch

White resigned. Black's sacrifice was gradually assuming more and more sinister overtones. Now, suddenly, on a board crowded with pieces, White discovers that he has no decent moves left at all. Everything he plays leads to disaster. He is totally paralysed – a fantastic circumstance. In chess terms this paralysis (which normally only occurs in the endgame) is known by the German word *Zugzwang*, which means compulsion to move. White is utterly blockaded. Let us look at the possibilities:

(a) If White plays 26 ♖d1 or 26 ♖c1 then ... ♖e2 wins White's queen.

(b) If White plays 26 ♔h2 then ... ♖5f3 also wins White's queen, since the bishop on g2 is pinned to the white king.

(c) If White plays 26 g4 then ... ♖5f3 27 ♗xf3 ♖h2 is checkmate.

(d) If White plays 26 ♗c1 then ... ♗xb1 wins material.

All other moves of White's pieces similarly allow them to be captured. White can postpone the end by playing h4 and a3, but eventually, he runs out of pawn moves. Black merely marks time by playing ... a5 and then ... ♔h7–g8–h7 etc., until the time comes when White must throw himself on the sword. This incredible game has been hailed as the 'Immortal Zugzwang Game'. Chess is a game symbolic of warfare. Once this is accepted, is it too fanciful to imagine that Nimzowitsch's conduct of this wonderful game was influenced by the trench warfare, the blockades which characterized World War 1?

Indian Defences

The Nimzo-Indian is as popular against 1 d4 as is the Sicilian against 1 e4. The defence is named after, and was indeed invented by, the Latvian Grandmaster, Aron Nimzowitsch. Nimzowitsch was active mainly during the 1920s and early 1930s and for much of this time was considered a candidate for the World Chess Championship. Nimzowitsch belonged to the Hypermodern School which held, amongst other tenets, that control of the centre need not derive solely from occupation with pawns. An acceptable alternative lay in permitting one's opponent to construct a strong pawn centre, which could then be undermined. The opening moves of the Nimzo-Indian (or Nimzowitsch-Indian, in its full form) are 1 d4 ♘f6 2 c4 e6 3 ♘c3 ♗b4. It is evident from this sequence that part of Black's undermining process will consist of inflicting targets on White's pawn structure by playing ... ♗xc3+ at some point to double White's pawns in the c-file. The so-called 'Indian' defences (including the Nimzo- and Queen's Indian) were introduced mainly during the 1920s. The appellation refers to a supposed resemblance to the Indian form of chess where players hold back the

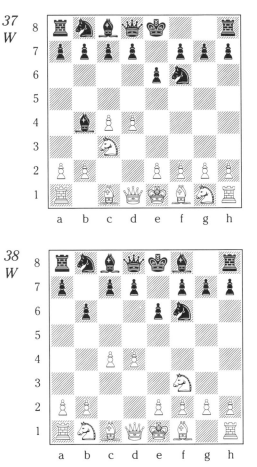

37
W

38
W

moves of their central pawns. The Nimzo-Indian is one of the most popular openings, numbering amongst its adherents Botvinnik, Capablanca, Fischer and Karpov.

9

RUSSIAN REVOLUTION

Botvinnik–Capablanca (Rotterdam 1938)

MIKHAIL BOTVINNIK was the first Soviet citizen to hold the World Championship. In this sense he was the founder of his nation's domination of world chess. Since 1948, when he took the title, all World Champions save Bobby Fischer have hailed from the USSR.

Botvinnik's talents were recognized in 1931 when he won the Soviet Championship. In 1936 he was regarded as a national hero when he won the Nottingham tournament with Capablanca. At the death of World Champion Alekhine, Botvinnik was widely regarded as his natural successor, but there was a two year delay before five players, Botvinnik, Smyslov, Keres, Reshevsky and Euwe, were selected to compete for the title in 1948. The five-way challenge was organized by the International Chess Federation, FIDE, which had been founded in 1924, but which had never before been involved in organizing the World Championship. Previous champions had treated the title as private property and had negotiated their own conditions for challenge matches. Botvinnik himself once told me that 'when you are World Champion you treat the title as though you own it and you cannot believe that it will fall into someone else's hands'.

For Botvinnik the unbelievable was to happen – he has the unique distinction of losing the title on no fewer than three occasions. He was briefly dethroned by Smyslov in 1957, but regained the title the following year. In 1960 he lost the championship to Tal and retook it in 1961. He surrendered the palm for the last time to Petrosian in 1963 and in 1970 retired from professional play. Throughout his heyday Botvinnik appeared as *primus inter pares*, never dominating his contemporaries in the

Mikhail Botvinnik

way that his predecessors Steinitz, Lasker, Capablanca and Alekhine had done. By the time of Botvinnik's reign there had been a tremendous upsurge in the quantity of top Grandmasters, promoted partly by the resources poured into chess by the Soviet authorities in their pursuit of world cultural and sporting excellence.

Botvinnik himself contributed to the Soviet phenomenon. His training methods and research findings became the accepted norm in his homeland. His chess school has trained some of the greatest players in the Soviet Union in recent years, including Kasparov, who became the youngest ever World Champion in 1985, at the age of 22.

Botvinnik stressed that chess required immense preparation and not just over the board inspiration. He was also the first to suggest that chess training should be physical and not just intellectual. Many people regard chess as a cerebral activity detached from bodily exertion but, in an arduous tournament or match, players can become physically exhausted.

Botvinnik detested the smell of tobacco and felt that he was distracted by the pipes and cigarettes of his opponents. His determination to succeed is well illustrated by the method he devised to overcome this weakness. He arranged private training sessions where his trainer, Ragozin, smoked constantly and blew smoke into his eyes. It might have been simpler to lobby FIDE to ban smoking in chess tournaments, as is now the accepted practice.

The game I have chosen was played against Capablanca in Rotterdam in 1938. Botvinnik was, at that time, the up and coming representative of the Soviet School of chess. Capablanca was the legendary figure, almost impossible to defeat, who represented the very best in chess of the previous three decades. This game, therefore, took on the symbolic overtone of a battle of generations of past and future champions. In fact, after this game, Botvinnik's ascent to the world title was blocked for ten years by the Second World War, while Capablanca never again performed at this exalted level, and had died of a heart attack within a matter of years.

White: Botvinnik
Black: Capablanca
Rotterdam 1938
NIMZO-INDIAN DEFENCE

A classic Botvinnik victory. Capablanca goes after a weak wing pawn and misplaces his queen. Botvinnik, with iron logic, presses on the kingside, makes more than a few problem-like moves and crushes his famous opponent. A game to replay and study.

1	d4	♘f6
2	c4	e6
3	♘c3	♗b4
4	e3	d5
5	a3	♗xc3+
6	bxc3	c5

7	cxd5	exd5
8	♗d3	0-0
9	♘e2	b6
10	0-0	♗a6

A fine idea if followed up correctly.

11	♗xa6	♘xa6
12	♗b2	

A strange-looking move, but not at all bad. More natural is 12 ♕d3 ♘c7 13 f3.

12	...	♕d7

If 12 ... c4 White will engineer an advantage with a future e4.

13	a4	

If 13 ♕d3, then 13 ♕a4.

13	...	♖fe8? *(39)*

Here the rook is misplaced. It belongs on c8, and e8 must be held in reserve as a haven for the retreat of Black's king's knight. Botvinnik himself states that 13 ... cxd4 14 cxd4 ♖fc8 would yield equality and that the text is an error.

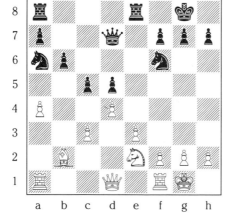

39
W

Jose Capablanca

14 ♕d3   c4

If 14 ... ♘c7 15 dxc5 bxc5 16 c4 with advantage to White. Reinfeld suggests 14 ... ♕b7.

15 ♕c2   ♘b8
16 ♖ae1

Preparing a central push and giving up the a-pawn, a profound plan which it is almost impossible to calculate completely.

16 ...   ♘c6
17 ♘g3   ♘a5

If 17 ... ♘e4, 18 ♘h1! followed by 19 f3, but certainly safer is Euwe's suggestion of 17 ... ♘e7.

18 f3   ♘b3
19 e4   ♕xa4
20 e5   ♘d7
21 ♕f2

Black threatened ... ♘bc5. Now White threatens ♘f5 with a strong attack.

21 ...   g6
22 f4   f5
23 exf6   ♘xf6
24 f5 *(40)*

Botvinnik's play is simple and brilliant.

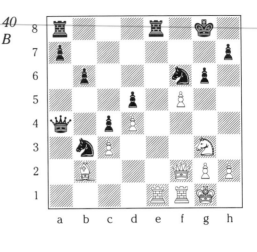

40
B

24 ...   ♖xe1
25 ♖xe1   ♖e8

Euwe suggests 25 ... ♘e4 as a stronger defence.

26 ♖e6!

A well calculated combination.

26 ...   ♖xe6

If 26 ... ♘e4 27 ♘xe4 dxe4 28 fxg6! and if 26 ... ♔f7 27 ♖xf6+ ♔xf6 28 fxg6+ ♔xg6 29 ♕f5+ ♔g7 30 ♘h5+ ♔h6 31 h4 ♖g8 32 g4 ♕c6 33 ♗a3! winning.

27 fxe6   ♔g7
28 ♕f4   ♕e8
29 ♕e5   ♕e7
30 ♗a3!! *(41)*

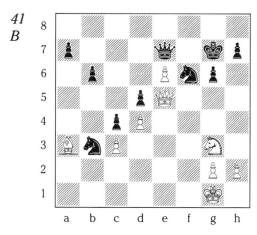

41
B

A delightful thrust creating, perhaps, the most celebrated position in the history of chess.

| 30 | ... | ♛xa3 |
| 31 | ♞h5+ *(42)* | |

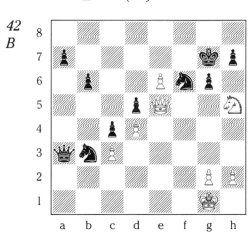

42
B

31	...	gxh5
32	♛g5+	♚f8
33	♛xf6+	♚g8
34	e7!	

Not 34 ♛f7+ ♚h8 35 e7 for the White d-pawn would be unprotected and Black gets a perpetual check.

34	...	♛c1+
35	♚f2	♛c2+
36	♚g3	♛d3+
37	♚h4	♛e4+
38	♚xh5	♛e2+
39	♚h4	♛e4+
40	g4	♛e1+
41	♚h5	

Black resigns. A superb game.

Larsen and Spassky

10

■ ■

THE RAMPANT ROOK

Larsen–Spassky (Belgrade 1970)

I N 1972 THE mild mannered Russian Boris Spassky sprang into public prominence as he tussled in Reykjavik to defend his world crown against the
mercurial and unpredictable American challenger, Bobby Fischer. Spassky
was born in Leningrad where as a child he studied chess for five hours every day in the
Palace of Young Pioneers. He won the Soviet Junior Championship in 1955 and the
Soviet Championship in 1961. He first challenged the wily Armenian Tigran Petrosian,
unsuccessfully as it turned out, for the World Championship in 1966. Three years later
he wrested the title from the same opponent in Moscow. In that second encounter
Spassky displayed his finest attacking style. Spassky also won many tournaments,
including Moscow 1964, the 1966 Piatigorsky Cup and Leiden 1970.

According to expert opinion Spassky can be ranked as the 8th strongest player
of all time. Before his 1972 defence of his world title against Fischer, he looked in
strong form, never having lost to Fischer during their previous encounters. Spassky's
defeat in the World Championship match of 1972 skewed his chess powers off
trajectory. His results thereafter appeared anodyne and lacklustre. He participated in
subsequent World Championship Candidates cycles, but failed to reach the final stage
of challenging for the world title. In 1974 he lost to the young Karpov, in 1977 he was
defeated by Korchnoi and in 1980 lost on tie break against the Hungarian Lajos
Portisch. In 1985 at Montpellier he did not even get to the final play-offs.

At the zenith of his powers Spassky's play was glittering and elegant. He was
regarded as the universal player, who could handle any type of position with insight
and supreme grasp of technique. In the following game from 1970, Spassky led the

USSR team in their conquest of the World in Belgrade. Billed as the 'Match of the Century' this was an important benchmark. The four round match demonstrated the complete domination of Soviet chess might, able to defeat the rest of the world over no fewer than ten boards. The final score was 20½ to the Soviets and 19½ to the world, whose team included Fischer, Larsen, Portisch, Hort and Gligoric. The Match was played in the Belgrade Trades Union Hall, where fluorescent lighting had been especially installed at Fischer's request. He also demanded that no photographs be taken during play, that the players would not talk during the rounds and that spectators should be seated at least 25 feet from the players. All these stipulations, quite unusual for chess tournaments at that time, were, nevertheless, carried out by the organisers.

Surprisingly Fischer was content to take board 2 for the World, behind Bent Larsen, the Danish Grandmaster. Larsen believed that his own results over the previous 18 months had been superior to the American's. In response Fischer declared 'I want to co-operate'. Could his unaccustomed modesty have been occasioned by his poor record against Spassky, whom he had, up to then, never been able to beat? Perhaps Fischer was saving himself for a more important occasion.

Larsen was one of the first modern western Grandmasters to pose a serious challenge to Soviet domination of the international circuit in the 1960s. In 1956, his outstanding result as top board for the Danish Olympic team in 1956 had persuaded him to give up his studies as a civil engineer and to become a professional chess player. Larsen has been a Candidate for the World Championship four times. He is still a popular and entertaining figure and has taken first prize in many tournaments, including London in 1989.

White: Larsen
Black: Spassky
The World versus the USSR Team Match, Belgrade 1970
NIMZO-LARSEN ATTACK

1	b3	e5
2	♗b2	♘c6
3	c4	♘f6
4	♘f3	

A risky and provocative move. Safer would be 4 e3.

4	...	e4
5	♘d4	♗c5
6	♘xc6	dxc6 (43)

Black sacrifices his pawn structure, allowing double pawns and capturing away from the centre, for the sake of speedy development. It is worth comparing the game Paulsen–Morphy early in the book for a similar example.

Spassky and Larsen

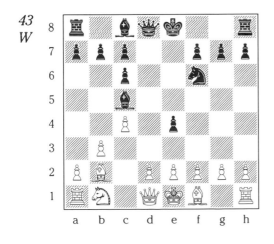

43
W

7	e3		♗f5
8	♕c2		♕e7
9	♗e2		0-0-0
10	f4?		

This move represents an almost imperceptible weakening of White's king's wing. Nevertheless, it requires play of genius on Spassky's part to expose this move as a mistake.

10	...		♘g4
11	g3		h5

12 h3   h4! *(44)*

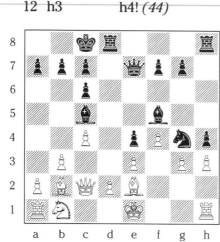

This move plays the role of John the Baptist. It is a great move, already sacrificing a piece to blast away the pawn protection around White's king. However, Black's 12th move is, in reality, simply a herald announcing a superstar move to come.

13 hxg4   hxg3
14 ♖g1

White is a piece up: how can Black penetrate his defences?

14 ...   ♖h1!! *(45)*

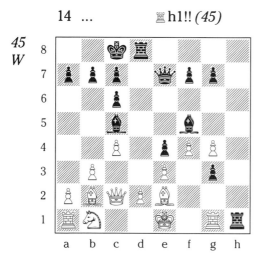

This rook swoop is one of the most fantastic moves ever played in a game of chess. Its effect is stunning. White must capture the rook but then Black gains access to the h4 square with his queen, with check. This invasion by the black queen is sufficient to annihilate White's resistance.

15 ♖xh1   g2
16 ♖f1

If White seeks to preserve the extra rook with 16 ♖g1 then Black wins with 16 ... ♕h4+ 17 ♔d1 ♕h1 18 ♖xh1 gxh1(=♕)+ 19 ♗f1 ♕xf1 checkmate.

16 ...   ♕h4+
17 ♔d1   gxf1(=♕)+ *(46)*

White resigns. After 18 ♗xf1 ♗xg4+ 19 ♗e2 ♕h1 is checkmate. Alternatively, 18 ♗xf1 ♗xg4+ 19 ♔c1 ♕e1+ 20 ♕d1 ♕xd1 checkmate.

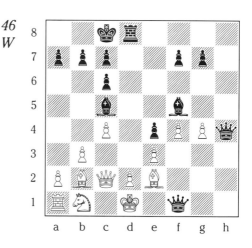

11

■ ■

A MOZART SYMPHONY

Fischer–Spassky (6th Match Game, Reykjavik 1972)

T HE 11th WORLD CHAMPION was Bobby Fischer – the brash unschooled teenager from Brooklyn, who toppled the might of the Soviet chess system before his 30th birthday. His story epitomized the self-reliant, frontier ideals of modern America and provided the inspiration for the Tim Rice/Abba musical CHESS. But the dream evaporated after Fischer stormed Soviet chess domination and took the world title from Spassky in 1972. Inexplicably he renounced chess totally and from that day, 19 years ago, has not played a single competitive game. He has not even visited a chess club or chess event as a spectator. Having reached the pinnacle of achievement perhaps he had nothing more to prove to himself or to the world. His self-imposed exile recalls the seclusion of the only other American to earn World Championship status – Paul Morphy.

His match against Spassky was characterized by the American's detailed demands and his near refusal to play before the match was even underway. Spassky had never lost a game to his antagonist and his meticulous pre-match preparation, both mental and physical (Spassky enjoyed playing tennis to keep fit), was well known. Spassky won the first game and was awarded the second by default, when Fischer failed to put in an appearance at the board.

Once Fischer had condescended to play, he employed a vast battery of psychological pressures, protesting about both the playing conditions and the board. He demanded the exclusive use of his hotel swimming pool and insisted that the official chess board be reduced in size by three millimetres. In retaliation the Soviet delegation alleged that Spassky was being distracted by electronic or chemical

Boris Spassky

equipment and demanded a complete search of the playing hall, including an X-ray of the players' chairs, which revealed that they contained two dead flies. The ballyhoo ended with Fischer taking the title $12\frac{1}{2}$–$8\frac{1}{2}$.

Inevitably a clash between representatives of Russia and America became overladen with symbolic and political overtones, which attracted the glare of the world media. Perhaps the western media exposure, to which Spassky, being a Russian, was quite unaccustomed, helped to knock the stuffing out of him. After 1972 chess enthusiasts witnessed an amazing and unexpectedly permanent decline in his morale. He never staged a comeback and his reputation was rapidly eclipsed by that of his younger compatriot, Anatoly Karpov. Spassky had previously conformed to the Soviet ideal of the sportsman, but now he found the restrictions of Soviet life tedious and applied for permission to emigrate. This was at a time when the Soviet authorities were tentatively relaxing restrictions on artistic figures such as Rostropovich, who was allowed to settle in the West. Spassky too was granted permission to represent Soviet culture abroad and he chose to join his French-born third wife, Marina, in her homeland. He now represents his adopted country in team events. However, Spassky's tournament results are hampered by strings of featureless games, agreed drawn without any real struggle.

Strangely, the 1972 match had an even more disastrous impact, in chess terms, on its victor. Fischer's self-imposed exile has angered and exasperated chess enthusiasts and the general public alike. It seems just one more capricious exploit by the most demanding and volatile star that chess has ever known.

Yet Fischer's apparently endless demands acted as a major catalyst in improving the lot of the professional chess player. In 1969 Spassky's World Championship prize had been $1,600. In 1972 the prize fund had been boosted to an unprecedented $250,000. In 1987, the prize fund for the Seville Kasparov-Karpov match was no less than £1.2 million. This was a development that came from Fischer's insistence that he should be remunerated on the same scale as other international celebrity sportsmen.

Fischer demonstrated, almost overnight, that chess was not just a cerebral activity for ageing intellectuals. He endowed the game with the mass appeal in the West that it had always enjoyed in the Soviet Union. Moreover he showed that chess players could make headline news and that the game could reward individual effort. There was a massive upsurge in the popularity of chess, which still has continuing effects some two decades later.

The game I have chosen was instrumental in deciding the outcome of the 1972 World Championship match.

White: Fischer
Black: Spassky
World Championship, 6th match game, Reykjavik 1972
QUEEN'S GAMBIT DECLINED

1	c4	e6
2	♘f3	d5
3	d4	♘f6
4	♘c3	♗e7
5	♗g5	0-0
6	e3	h6
7	♗h4	b6

This is the Tartakower Variation, really a modernized version of the old Orthodox Defence to the Queen's Gambit. According to theory it is playable. Spassky has used it often before and it is currently a favourite of both Karpov and Kasparov.

8	cxd5	♘xd5
9	♗xe7	♕xe7
10	♘xd5	exd5
11	♖c1	♗e6

This is the paradoxical point of the Tartakower Variation. One might have expected 11 ... ♗b7 here, but in fact the bishop is better placed on e6.

12	♕a4	c5
13	♕a3	♖c8
14	♗b5	a6? (47)

An improvement found later is 14 ... ♕b7 15 dc bc 16 ♖xc5 ♖xc5 17 ♕xc5 ♘a6! with good play for the pawn (Timman–Geller, Hilversum 1973).

47
W

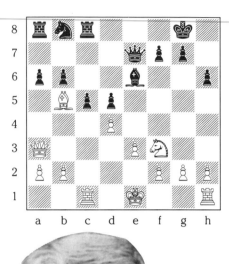

Bobby Fischer

15	dxc5	bxc5
16	0-0	♖a7
17	♗e2	♘d7
18	♘d4	

A clever use of the pin to improve the position of his pieces; Fischer is playing with wonderful finesse.

18	...	♕f8
19	♘xe6	fxe6
20	e4! *(48)*	

A beautifully incisive move which reminds one in a forthright way that White is a player in the great American tradition in a direct line from Morphy, via Pillsbury to Capablanca. Black will now have to yield up command of at least one diagonal.

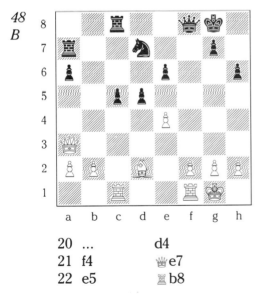

20	...	d4
21	f4	♕e7
22	e5	♖b8

After the game, at dinner that night, the great Argentinian Grandmaster, Miguel Najdorf showed a line that he thought would have given Black a

good game starting off with 22 ... ♘b6 with the idea of playing ... ♘d5. But this is defeated by 23 ♕b3 and if 23 ... ♘d5 24 f5, or as ex-World Champion Tal subsequently pointed out, an immediate 23 f5, since 23 ... exf5 loses the knight after 24 ♕b3 + .

23	♗c4	♔h8
24	♕h3	♘f8
25	b3	a5 *(49)*

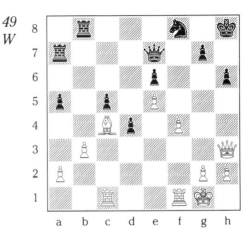

Now comes the breakthrough on the f-file that enables White to drive a wedge in the Black position.

26	f5	exf5
27	♖xf5	♘h7
28	♖cf1	♕d8
29	♕g3	♖e7
30	h4	♖bb7
31	e6	♖bc7
32	♕e5	♕e8
33	a4	♕d8
34	♖1f2	♕e8
35	♖2f3	♕d8
36	♗d3	♕e8
37	♕e4	♘f6

Spassky and Fischer, Reykjavik 1972

38	♖xf6	gxf6
39	♖xf6	♚g8
40	♗c4	♚h8
41	♕f4 *(50)*	Black resigned

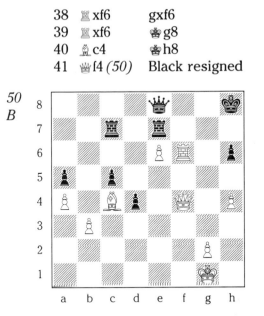

50
B

The only means of averting ♖f8+ is 41 ... ♚g8 to which Fischer intended replying 42 ♕xh6.

Widely accepted as the best game from the famous match which swept Fischer to the world title, this was described by Miguel Najdorf as the chess equivalent of a Mozart symphony, a comment which went round the world at that time.

Kasparov, Larsen and Karpov

12

■ ■

STAR WARS

Karpov–Kasparov (Moscow 1985)

I N 1975, THE YOUTHFUL RUSSIAN, Anatoly Karpov, became the first man in history to win the World Championship by default. Bobby Fischer's refusal to play astounded the chess world and left the victor with a determination to prove himself worthy of the crown. As Champion, Karpov energetically established a record for winning first prizes in tournaments (at the moment his tally is some 80 tournament first places).

Karpov learnt to play chess at the age of 4 and won the World Junior Championship in 1969, three points ahead of the rest of the field. A year later he gained his Grandmaster title in Venezuela. On the way to his world title in 1975 Karpov defeated such opponents as Polugayevsky, Spassky and Korchnoi. Twice, in 1978 and again in 1981, he fought off a challenge from the great Victor Korchnoi. But after a decade of autocratic dominance Karpov met his nemesis in the shape of the young Azerbaijani, Gary Kasparov. The challenger was a product of the Botvinnik school of chess. Kasparov had become a Grandmaster at the astonishing age of 17, in 1980, and experts already predicted that he would be even stronger than Fischer.

Between 1984 and 1990 Karpov played the almost incredible total of five matches against Kasparov for the title. The first match was unique in chess annals in being abandoned unfinished after five and a half months and 48 games, no fewer than 40 of them drawn! Controversy still surrounds the decision of Florencio Campomanes, the President of FIDE, to halt the match on the official grounds that both players were exhausted. But Kasparov had just won the 47th and 48th games and seemed to have cracked the secret of beating his mighty opponent.

Their 1985 encounter was limited to 24 games and Kasparov scored 13 points to his opponent's 11 to become, at the age of 22, the youngest World Champion ever. Karpov's right to a revenge match was exercised in 1986, the centenary of the first World Championship between Steinitz and Zukertort. Karpov went down again with a score of $11\frac{1}{2}$ to Kasparov's $12\frac{1}{2}$.

These perpetual antagonists met again the following year in Seville, when the match was drawn and thus Kasparov retained his title. They then met once more at the end of 1990 in a two-centre match at New York and Lyons, Kasparov narrowly winning $12\frac{1}{2}$–$11\frac{1}{2}$.

The rivalry between these two men is heightened by their different styles on and off the chessboard. Karpov is a pillar of establishment Soviet society, a young pioneer, whose hobbies include stamp collecting. Kasparov is the buccaneer, an advocate of *perestroika* and *glasnost* even before the advent of Gorbachev's regime, he is now one of the fiercest critics of the failure of the Gorbachev regime to achieve full democracy.

The game which decided the second Karpov–Kasparov match in 1985 was

Kasparov and Karpov

superb. Everything hung on this final game. If Karpov won he stayed as champion. If Kasparov won he would become the youngest World Champion in the history of chess. The game itself witnessed an attack described by David Bronstein as 'outstandingly brilliant, one of the most impressive in the 100 years of the championship'. The middlegame offensive was so recondite that Grandmaster experts in the Moscow press room were, at first, quite baffled by the depth of Black's concept. As the match started, I had described Karpov as 'essentially repressive' and Kasparov as 'basically revolutionary' in their respective approaches to the solution of chessboard problems. Towards the end I amplified this: 'in Moscow the conflict is currently seen as one of materialism versus sacrifice. Time after time, Kasparov has sacrificed pieces ... to launch a devastating attack. In sharp contrast Karpov had to entrench himself and absorb the shock tactics'. Watch now as this symbolic and supremely exciting battle of opposing chessboard styles unfolds.

White: Karpov
Black: Kasparov
World Championship, 24th match game, Moscow 1985
SICILIAN DEFENCE.

1	e4	c5

Requiring only a draw, Kasparov still selects the sharpest possible defence against White's opening move.

2	♞f3	d6
3	d4	cxd4
4	♞xd4	♞f6
5	♞c3	a6
6	♗e2	e6
7	0-0	♗e7
8	f4	0-0
9	♔h1	♛c7
10	a4	♞c6
11	♗e3	♖e8
12	♗f3	♖b8
13	♛d2	♗d7

14	♞b3	b6
15	g4	

This position had already occurred in the match, but Karpov's 15th move constitutes an aggressive thrust which is a new departure for him. The disadvantage is that this pawn move leaves a vacuum in its wake which may present a future source of weakness.

15	...	♗c8
16	g5	♞d7
17	♛f2 *(51)*	

Varying from the game Sokolov–Ribli, just played at the Montpellier Candidates' tournament and published in Moscow only two days before this game. There White tried 17 ♗g2 which was met by 17 ... ♞a5. Karpov tried to improve White's conduct of the attack.

51
B

17	...	♗f8
18	♗g2	♗b7
19	♖ad1	g6
20	♗c1	♖bc8

This is not best. Black should play 20 ... ♘c5!

21 ♖d3

Introducing an apparently crude, but nevertheless dangerous, attacking scheme.

21	...	♘b4
22	♖h3	♗g7
23	♗e3?	

White hopes to follow up with ♕h4 and f4–f5, but his slow offensive is hampered by the distance of his knights from the main scene of action. Very dangerous is 23 f5!

Kasparov and Karpov

23	...	♖e7
24	♔g1	♖ce8! (52)

Kasparov's defence is extremely profound, culminating in this apparently mysterious massing of his rooks in the confined spaces of the closed king's file. The main idea is to discourage White from playing f4–f5 when the answer ... e6xf5 will permit Black's rooks to rampage down the newly opened central file.

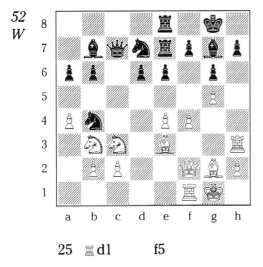

52 W

25	♖d1	f5

Kasparov breaks out and his rooks soon begin to play their part in his counterattack. The text involves an imaginative sacrifice of his b-pawn.

26	gxf6	♘xf6
27	♖g3	

If immediately 27 ♗xb6, then either 27 ... ♕b8, as in the game, or even 27 ... ♘g4.

27	...	♖f7
28	♗xb6	♕b8

29	♗e3	♘h5
30	♖g4	♘f6
31	♖h4	

Karpov should have retreated with 31 ♖g3, but this would have allowed 31 ... ♘h5 drawing by repetition of moves and giving Kasparov the title. Striving to avoid this disaster, Karpov stumbles into a brilliant new sacrifice, curiously of Black's other knight's pawn.

31	...	g5!! (53)

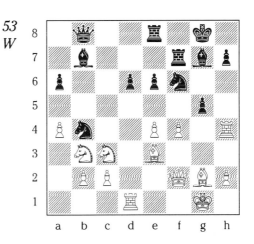

53 W

An unexpected blow that sweeps the remaining shackles from Black's forces. In the last few minutes of play, with the World Champion in desperate time trouble, the White position is now utterly routed.

32	fxg5	♘g4
33	♕d2	♘xe3
34	♕xe3	♘xc2
35	♕b6	♗a8
36	♖xd6?	

This loses a piece. 36 ♕xb8 ♖xb8 37 ♗h3! was forced.

36	...	♖b7
37	♕xa6	♖xb3

Also rushed for time, Kasparov misses the crushing 37 ... ♘b4!

38	♖xe6	♖xb2
39	♕c4	

Threatening mate on e8 which Kasparov sidesteps.

39	...	♚h8
40	e5	♕a7+
41	♚h1	♗xg2+
42	♚xg2	♘d4+ *(54)*

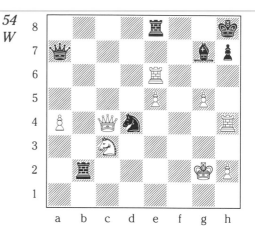

54
W

White now resigned the game and the title.

Raymond Keene and Kasparov

94

The Sicilian Defence

This defence, perhaps the most popular against the king's pawn, commences after the moves 1 e4 c5 (55). Its name stems from the Sicilian Priest, Pietro Carrera, who published the defence in 1617. Carrera, not much noted as a player, derives his main claim to fame from his recording of the new openings employed by the Italian masters of the late 16th century such as Greco, Polerio and Salvio.

The most ferocious variation of the Sicilian is the Dragon Variation, which arises after the common sequence: 1 e4 c5 2 ♘f3 d6 3 d4 cxd4 4 ♘xd4 ♘f6 5 ♘c3 g6. The name derives from the shape of Black's pawn structure which is said, fancifully, to resemble the outline of a dragon. More than 25% of all master games are Sicilians, and the vast popularity of this opening resides in the opportunities it grants Black for counterattack, rather than pure defence. Although regarded with suspicion from the 1850s to the mid-1930s, the Sicilian Defence has been championed by Staunton, Botvinnik, Tal, Fischer and Kasparov.

55
W

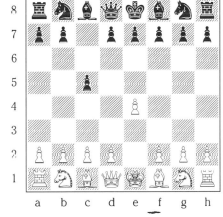

LIST OF ILLUSTRATIONS

All illustrations are from the archives of B. T. Batsford, except where indicated.

Anderssen	16	New York 1934	61
Kieseritsky (British Chess Magazine)	19	Nimzowitsch (Gareth Williams)	64
Morphy	23	Sämisch (Gareth Williams)	67
Paulsen (Gareth Williams)	25	Botvinnik	70
Zukertort	28	Capablanca	73
Blackburne	29	Larsen and Spassky	76
Tchigorin	36	Spassky and Larsen	79
Steinitz	37	Spassky	83
Pillsbury	42	Fischer	84
Lasker	47	Spassky and Fischer	87
Capablanca and Lasker (Hulton-Deutsch)	50	Kasparov, Larsen and Karpov	88
Bern 1932	52	Kasparov and Karpov	90
Bogolyubov (Gareth Williams)	56	Kasparov and Karpov	92
Alekhine	59	Keene and Kasparov	94

The back cover photograph of Raymond Keene is by Mark Huba; that of Donald Woods by The Hulton Picture Company.